Table of Contents

Preface:

The purpose of this work is twofold. First, it aims to provide an introduction to the social history of the German pioneers in America. Second, it aims for this history to serve as the means for greater understanding of German-Americans and their way of life.

DHT

Introduction:

"Portsch" - that is the way my Father always pronounced and spelled the English word "porch," and in response to those monolingual Americans who would say to him, "That is not the way it is spelled in Webster's dictionary," my Father would always calmly state, "Well, Webster is wrong."

This is only one tiny example of the many ways I became aware of, as I grew up, that people of different backgrounds have different ways of looking at things, or a different *Weltanschauung*. Various ethnic groups have their own customs, traditions, and ways of doing, saying and thinking about life.

As there is no uniformity in terms of ethnicity in the U.S., but rather a rich mosaic of various ethnic groups, it is important to understand and appreciate them all. (1) An appropriate point of departure in this regard is to understand lifestyle, customs, traditions, etc., since these constitute the basic elements of ethnicity.

As the nation's largest ethnic group, it is of necessity important to examine the *Weltanschauung* of the German-American element. (2) Of course, this is easier said than done, as this element itself is a diverse group derived from immigrants who came from Germany, Austria, Switzerland, Luxemburg, and other German-speaking regions of Europe. Regardless of the strong regional particularisms, there is nevertheless, obviously much that is held in common.

To understand the German-American heritage it is necessary to examine the social history of German-Americans, as it best displays all that can be understood in terms of their *Weltanschauung*. Where to begin? The best place to begin is in the very beginnings of German-American history, especially in Pennsylvania where the German element first concentrated in substantial numbers, and where German-American community life and institutions first began to develop substantially.

In the 19th century, German-Americans would begin to try to articulate what Germandom was all about. In 1871, Carl Ruemelin of Cincinnati attempted to define it by asking:

"Does Germandom consist of daily sitting together in social intercourse at the beer table? Or the friendly drinking of Rhine wine together? Is it German fare in the family circle? Is it in the culture of the vine or the cultivation of the fields? Or is it to be found, as has been long believed, in the ritual of the churches, conducted in the German language, since a deeply religious quality has been ascribed to it? Or is Germandom anchored in position by the German newspapers or by their adjutants, the popular German political addresses? Or is it by singing, athletic and workingmen's clubs that German life is most efficiently fostered? Or is it the official recognition of the German language in the printing of official documents and in school instruction?" (3)

Although he does not answer the question, it is obvious that Ruemelin felt that all these elements were part of what it meant for him to be a German-American. Part of being a German-American was, as Carl Schurz, noted in his well known definition, that it should blend "the best parts of the American spirit and melt these with the best parts of the German spirit." (4)

W.A. Fritisch expressed his definition of German-Americanism by advising Germans to: 1. Speak German at home and enroll children in German instruction, and send them to German-American churches; 2. Cooperate together for the establishment of schools with German instruction; 3. Read German-langage newspapers; 4. Make sure that there are new and good German books at your local public library; 5. Participate actively in political affairs; and, 6. Celebrate German-American Day annually. (5)

By the 20th century, German-American intellectuals, such as H.L. Mencken, Hugo Muensterberg, Kuno Francke, G.S. Viereck, and others, wrote numerous works dealing with various aspects of the German-American *Weltanschauung*, and all of these should be taken into consideration, but as a German-American social history has yet to be written, the editor felt that it would be appropriate to make a contribution to this history by looking at the colonial period and examining the beginnings of German-American social history. (6)

To accomplish this task, the editor has selected two works which deal with German pioneer life in America. First, there is the work by Benjamin Rush, which is considered a "classic" in the field of German-American Studies, and, second, the lesser known work of Schantz, which supplements and complements the former.

Notes:

1. An excellent introductory history of American ethnic groups can be found in Roger Daniels, *Coming to America: A History of Immigration and Ethnicity in American Life*, (New York: HarperCollins Publishers, 1990).

2. According to the 1990 U.S. Census, the German-American element constitutes the nation's largest ethnic group at sixty millions, or one-fourth of the total population.

3. Cited in Herman W. Ronnenberg, *The Politics of Assimilation: The Effect of Prohibition on the German-Americans*, (New York: Carlton Pr., 1975), p 21.

4. For references to publications dealing with Schurz, see Don Heinrich Tolzmann, *Catalog of the German-Americana Collection, University of Cincinnati*, (Munich: K.G. Saur, 1990).

5. For further information on Fritsch, see Don Heinrich Tolzmann, "An Indiana German Historian," *Indiana German Heriage Society Newsletter*, 1:4(1985): 26.

6. The works of these German-American intellectuals can be found listed in Tolzmann, *Catalog*.

1. German Pioneer Lifestyle

By

Benjamin Rush

This section is a facsimile of material which appeared originally as: Benjamin Rush, "An Account of the Manners of the German Inhabitants of Pennsylvania. Introduction and Annotations by Theodore E. Schmauk. Notes by I. Daniel Rupp, revised," *Pennsylvania German Society Proceedings and Addresses*, 19(1910): 3-128.

CONTENTS.

INTRODUCTION.

RUSH'S ACCOUNT OF THE GERMANS.

PREFATORY NOTE.

This classical essay of Dr. Rush, taken from his works, would have appeared last year, on the One Hundred and Twentieth Anniversary of its original publication, had it been possible for the writer to complete the annotations in time.

Material not otherwise credited may in general be ascribed to the undersigned, and illustrations to Dr. J. F. Sachse.

Theodore E. Schmauk

WORKS ON BENJAMIN RUSH.

The following list contains the biographical works alluded to in the present volume:

AN EULOGIUM IN MEMORY OF THE LATE DR. BENJAMIN RUSH. Delivered and Published at the Request of the Graduates and Students of Medicine in the University of Pennsylvania, by William Staughton, D.D. Philadelphia, 1813.

ELEGIAC POEM ON THE DEATH OF DR. BENJAMIN RUSH. Philadelphia, 1813.

AN EULOGIUM UPON BENJAMIN RUSH, M.D. Written at the Request of the Medical Society of South Carolina. By David Ramsay, M.D. Philadelphia, Bradford and Inskeep, 1813.

AN INTRODUCTORY DISCOURSE TO A COURSE OF LECTURES ON THE THEORY AND PRACTICE OF PHYSICS, AND A TRIBUTE TO THE MEMORY OF THE LATE DR. BENJAMIN RUSH. Delivered at the College of Physicians and Surgeons (New York), on the Third of November, 1813, by David Hasock, M.D., F.L.S. New York, 1813.

BIOGRAPHICAL MEMORIAL OF DR. BENJAMIN RUSH. From Evangelical Repository, by Ebenezer Harlow Cummins. Philadelphia, February, 1816. Vol. I., No. 2.

LIFE OF BENJAMIN RUSH. By J. Sanderson. Sandersons' Biography of the Signers. Vol. IV. Philadelphia, 1820–1827. (Illustr. ed., 1865).

NATIONAL PORTRAIT GALLERY OF DISTINGUISHED AMERICANS. Vol. III. Philadelphia, 1836.

THE CHARACTER OF RUSH. AN INTRODUCTION TO THE COURSE ON MEDICINE, IN THE PHILADELPHIA COLLEGE OF MEDICINE (March, 1848). By Thomas D. Mitchell, Professor in the Philadelphia College of Medicine. Philadelphia, 1848.

SKETCH OF BENJAMIN RUSH. By H. D. Gilpin.

BENJAMIN RUSH. By William Pepper. An address before the American Medical Association at Newport, R. I., June, 1889. Chicago, 1890.

CRITICISM OF WM. B. REED'S ASPERSIONS ON THE CHARACTER OF DR. BENJAMIN RUSH. By a member of the Philadelphia Bar. (John G. Johnson.)

HISTORICAL NOTES OF DR. BENJAMIN RUSH. Mitchell. Pennsylvania Magazine. Philadelphia, 1903.

AN ADDRESS DELIVERED AT THE UNVEILING OF A MONUMENT BY THE AMERICAN MEDICAL ASSOCIATION TO THE MEMORY OF BENJAMIN RUSH IN WASHINGTON, by James Wilson, M.A., M.D., June 11, 1904. Philadelphia, J. B. Lippincott Company, 1904.

A MEMORIAL OF DR. BENJAMIN RUSH WRITTEN BY HIMSELF. Published privately by Louis Alexander Biddle. Lanorie, 1905. (Sign of the Ivy Leaf, Sansom Street, Philadelphia.)

HISTORICAL INTRODUCTION

INTRODUCTION.

I. The Author.

THE fathers of the Pennsylvania-Germans could have had no more distinguished eulogist than Dr. Benjamin Rush.[1] In peace and in war, in politics and in society, in legislation and in letters, in labors for the welfare of humanity, in pre-Revo-

[1] Bibliography.

Benjamin Rush was born in Bucks County, December 24, 1745. He was at the height of his career during his country's struggle for independence and during its first constitutional period. His essay on the German Inhabitants was written in 1789. He died, while still in the midst of affairs, on April 19, 1813. Contemporaries recognized his greatness, and his death immediately

lutionary and Post-Revolutionary activity, he was one of

---

called forth a number of biographies and eulogies. The earliest of these was at the request of the University of Pennsylvania, and was an address by Dr. Staughton, the Presbyterian minister in Philadelphia. A second was in the form of an Elegiac Poem, with clever lines, but in the most stilted and extravagant eighteenth century style, contrasting to a marked extent with the sobriety and poise of Dr. Rush's own writings. A third, and the best by far, for solid information and genuine insight, is the Eulogy written at the request of the South Carolina Medical Society by one of his former pupils and friends, Dr. David Ramsay. A fourth is found in a lecture delivered before the College of Physicians and Surgeons in New York by Dr. David Hasock.

In 1836, The National Portrait Gallery of Distinguished Americans published a life of Rush, with a fine full-page steel engraving, in its third volume, the material of which, however, depends upon the Eulogy by Ramsay mentioned above, and upon the Biography of the Signers of the Declaration of Independence. There is also a painting of Benjamin Rush executed by Charles Wilson Peale, a reproduction of which is found in Biddle, *Autobiography of Rush,* opposite p. 237; and a portrait of Rush by Sully in The Pennsylvania Hospital, Philadelphia.

In 1890 Provost William Pepper, of the University, made a thorough study of the life of Benjamin Rush.

In 1904, Dr. James Wilson, of Jefferson Medical College, Philadelphia, delivered a discriminative address on Benjamin Rush at the unveiling of the monument to the latter, in Washington, D. C.

The fullest and most important, as well as the most recent life of Dr. Benjamin Rush, is that privately published by Louis Alexander Biddle, under the title "A Memorial of Dr. Benjamin Rush Written by Himself" (1905), which is devoted chiefly to the history of the Rush family and its founder, but which contains the extensive and valuable autobiographical diary of Dr. Rush.

the makers of the nation, and Pennsylvania had no more distinguished[2] citizen.[3]

The fullest collection of Rush titles is to be found in the Library of the Historical Society of Pennsylvania. The Philadelphia Library, founded by Franklin, the friend of Rush, strange to say, contains little biographical material worthy of this great Pennsylvanian, although some of the volumes of his diary, much mutilated, are in its possession; and the list of titles available at its Ridgway Branch, founded by the son of Dr. Benjamin Rush, who left a million dollars for this purpose, and named the library in honor of his wife, is not complete. The Ridgway Branch contains a large collection of manuscript letters written to Dr. Rush.

[2] FAME OF DR. RUSH.

"The name of Dr. Rush gave a splendor to the American character, and greatly added to its reputation throughout the republic of letters. His works are read coextensively with the language in which they are written, and are daily quoted as standard medical authority by the learned of different nations. . . . He has been one of the most prominent pillars, on which his country's claim to be ranked among learned nations has preeminently rested, ever since Franklin was no more."—Ramsay, *An Eulogium,* 1813, pp. 9–10.

In London, as a young man, Dr. Rush made the acquaintance of Benjamin West, Lord Macauley, and Oliver Goldsmith. Benjamin Franklin was his friend, and throughout his life in Philadelphia he moved on terms of intimacy with the leaders of the new Republic. In his Diary (Biddle, *Autobiography of Rush,* p. 81), he remarks, "John and Samuel Adams domesticated themselves in my family. . . . Patrick Henry was my patient under inoculation for the smallpox."

Shortly before his death, Dr. Rush effected a reconciliation between Thomas Jefferson and John Adams.—Johnson, p. 55. Jefferson in a letter to Adams, May 27, 1813, announcing Rush's death, said: "Another of our patriots of '76 is gone, my dear sir,

A graduate of Princeton,[4] and of the University of Edinburgh, a student in London and in Paris[5] under the tutelage of Franklin, who advanced means to pay his expenses, a professor of chemistry at the age of twenty-four, an advocate of the abolition of slavery, and one of the two organizers of the first anti-slavery society in America, a champion of colonial rights in pre-Revolu-

---

another of the Signers of the Independence of our country. And a better man than Rush could not have left us, more benevolent, more learned, of finer genius, or more honest."—Johnson, p. 50.

He also was intimate with Thomas Paine, though he did not approve of Paine's unbelief or of the dissoluteness of his life. He tells us, in his Diary, that it was he who, in conference with Paine, gave the title to Paine's "*Common Sense.*"

"He was great in the midst of greatness."—Staughton, *An Eulogium,* 1813.

"One of the most original and powerful men whom medicine has ever claimed for a son."—Richardson.

"He will remain forever with us . . . as the first of our great physicians."—Pepper.

"The first Great American Physician."—Wilson.

[3] Rush's preliminary draft of the Declaration of Independence, his writings in favor of Independence and of popular sovereignty, his critical and constructive work on the national and state Constitutions, his grappling with the problem of popular education, his inquiry into political, social, sanitary, criminal and other conditions, marked him as among the greatest of our citizens.

[4] The then President of Princeton, Dr. Finley, was his uncle, and took a deep personal interest in his education. While at Edinburgh, Rush became the medium of inducing Witherspoon to immigrate to America.

[5] He passed through his student days in this gay capital and other cities with unusual earnestness of purpose.

tionary movements,[6] the chairman of the Provincial Conference of Pennsylvania who reported that it had become expedient for Congress to declare independence, a member of the Continental Congress, and a signer of the Declaration of Independence,[7] a physician-general of the Revolutionary army, a moulder and an advocate of a Federal Constitution[8] for the Union, a member of the State

---

[6] "Rush was a member of the Provincial Conference of Pennsylvania, and with James Smith, served upon a committee to consider and report upon the question as to the expediency of the declaration of independence by Congress. The report of this committee, which is generally attributed to the pen of Rush, contained much that was incorporated into the Declaration, and urged that measure with great force."—Wilson, *Address in 1904*, p. 6.

[7] "The vote for independence taken in Congress on July 2, 1776, was given by Pennsylvania as three in favor, Franklin, Wilson and Morton, and two against, Willing and Humphreys. Franklin was the only one of the Pennsylvania delegation who voted for independence from the beginning; Dickinson and Robert Morris absented themselves from the voting. The Declaration of Independence, adopted July 4, was a public expression of the vote taken on July 2. The signatures were attached in August, and the Pennsylvania signers, owing to some changes in the delegation, made by the convention of July 20, were Robert Morris, Benjamin Rush, Benjamin Franklin, John Morton, George Clymer, James Smith, George Taylor, James Wilson and George Ross.—Barr Ferree, *Pennsylvania: A Primer,* 1904.

Rush's principle was, "No form of government can be rational, but that which is derived from the suffrage of the people who are the subjects of it."—Biddle, *Autobiography of Rush,* p. 26.

[8] Dr. Rush published four powerful Letters on the Pennsylvania Constitution of 1776, a remarkable address in 1785 entitled *Considerations on the Test Laws of Pennsylvania,* and many able

Convention to ratify this Federal Constitution, a framer of the constitution for the State of Pennsylvania,[9] an advocate of public schools before the time,[10] president

---

though short articles in 1786–1787 in favor of the adoption of the Federal Constitution.—Pepper. Dr. Rush, with prophetic insight, anticipated the verdict of posterity as to the Federal Constitution. He declared it to be "a masterpiece of human wisdom."

[9] His activity, and his series of letters on the Constitution of Pennsylvania, caused it to be changed through his influence.

[10] RUSH ON PUBLIC SCHOOLS.

Dr. Rush might well be termed the Father of the Public School Plan in America. The following is a list of his writings on the subject:

A PLAN FOR ESTABLISHING PUBLIC SCHOOLS in Pennsylvania, and for Conducting Education agreeably to a Republican Form of Government. Addressed to the Legislature and Citizens of Pennsylvania in the year 1786.—Rush, *Essays Literary, Moral,* etc.

THE MODE OF EDUCATION PROPER IN A REPUBLIC.—Rush, *Essays Literary, Moral,* etc.

OBSERVATIONS UPON THE STUDY of the Latin and Greek Languages as a Branch of Liberal Education, With Hints of a Plan of Liberal Instruction Without Them.—Rush, *Essays Literary, Moral,* etc.

THOUGHTS UPON FEMALE EDUCATION . . . in the United States of America.—Rush, *Essays Literary, Moral,* etc.

On this subject, Dr. Pepper (p. 10) remarks of Dr. Rush, "If time permitted, it would be easy to show that in the vital matter of education he was as active, as progressive and as far ahead of his contemporaries as he was in social science.

In 1786, "he addressed to the legislature of his own state, his memorable plan for the general diffusion of learning, which led the way for some of the most important educational provisions that have ever been devised or adopted in any country. So valu-

and secretary of the Pennsylvania Society for the Abolition of Slavery,[11] vice-president and a founder of the Philadelphia Bible Society,[12] a member of the American Philosophical Society, and treasurer of the United States Mint to the day of his death, Dr. Benjamin Rush, one hundred and twenty years ago, found the time, and felt it incumbent upon him not only to point out the sterling qualities of the German settlers in Pennsylvania, but also to call upon the "citizens of the United States"[13] to learn from these Germans "to prize knowledge and industry in agriculture and manufactures"; and upon

---

able and yet concise are his leading arguments in favor of general education, that I venture to quote them here."—Mitchell, p. 9,

[11] March 1, 1780, the first abolition act passed in America was adopted by the Assembly of Pennsylvania "for the gradual abolition of slavery." It had been originally proposed by Vice-President Bryan in 1778. It provided that "all negro children born after March 1, 1780, might be held in service until the age of 21 and no longer." It has been estimated that there were then in Pennsylvania about 4,000 slaves; the census of 1790 gives the number as 3,737; in 1820 they had decreased to about 200.

"In 1794 a convention of abolition societies was held in Philadelphia, with delegates from Connecticut, New York, New Jersey, Pennsylvania, Delaware and Maryland."—Barr Ferree, *Pennsylvania: A Primer,* 1904.

[12] The term "*Bible Society*" is said to have originated in Pennsylvania with Dr. Rush.

[13] Philadelphia was at this time the capital of the United States (1790–1800), and Dr. Rush, like Franklin, by his writings was a national character, and through his students who settled in all parts of the land was an authoritative adviser on public questions and a recognized disseminator of culture. "Dr. Rush was a public writer for forty-nine years, and from the nineteenth to the sixty-eighth year of his age."—Ramsay, *An Eulogium,* p. 97.

BIBLIA,

Das ist:

Die

Heilige Schrifft

Altes und Neues

Testaments,

Nach der Deutschen Uebersetzung

D. Martin Luthers,

Mit jedes Capitels kurtzen Summarien, auch beygef.ügten vielen und richtigen Parllelen;

Nebst einem Anhang

Des dritten und vierten Buchs Esra und des dritten Buchs der Maccabäer.

Germantown:

Gedruckt bey Christoph Saur, 1743.

REVISED TITLE PAGE OF THE SAUER BIBLE.

the legislators[14] of the United States to "learn from the wealth and independence of the German inhabitants of Pennsylvania, to encourage industry and economy, the only pillars which can support the present Constitution[15] of the United States."

Dr. Rush even felt it wise to admonish the lawmakers of Penn's commonwealth, to "learn from the history of your German fellow citizens, that you possess an inexhaustible treasure in the State *in their manners and arts.*" He foresaw the modern greatness of the German language; and said, "Do not contend with their prejudices in favor of their language. It will be the channel through which the knowledge and discoveries of the nations in Europe may be conveyed into our country. In proportion as they are instructed and enlightened in their *own* language, they will become acquainted with the language of the United States."

Dr. Rush was a Quaker descendant from a cavalry captain in Cromwell's army, who followed Penn to this country in 1683. His earliest instructor was his uncle, a clergyman who subsequently became president of Princeton College. He himself graduated from Princeton in

[14] "These great political subjects, for the time being, engrossed his whole soul—the independence of his country—the establishment of a good constitution for the United States, and for his own particular state—to enlighten the public mind and to diffuse correct ideas."—Ramsay, *An Eulogium,* p. 102.

[15] The Constitution went into effect on March 4, 1789, Dr. Rush himself being a member of the convention which ratified it; and it was in this very year 1789 that he wrote the treatise which forms the subject of this work.

2

VIEWS IN OLD PHILADELPHIA DURING DR. RUSH'S LIFE, showing the Court House and Quaker Meeting at Second and Market Sts. From a Contemporary Drawing in the Collection of Julius F. Sachse.

1760, studied medicine for six years[16] with a physician in Philadelphia, went to the University of Edinburgh for two years, spent another year in the hospitals of London and Paris, and at the age of twenty-four began to practice medicine, and teach chemistry in the Philadelphia Medical College.[16a] For the next twenty years he was most actively engaged in Revolutionary and American problems bearing on the reconstruction of the nation. In 1789, the year in which he wrote his "Account of the Germans in Pennsylvania," at the age of forty-four, be became lecturer on the theory and practice of physic, and two years later, in 1791, when the Medical College which he had helped to found merged into the University of Pennsylvania, he became professor of the institutes of medicine and of chemical practice in the university; and in 1805 was made its professor of the theory and practice of physic.

During the Revolution[17] Dr. Rush was in constant attendance on the wounded in the battles of Trenton,

---

[16] It is said that during this whole term of six years, there were only two days on which he missed attendance for any and every cause whatsoever.

[16a] "We find in the papers of the day, an imposing announcement of the arrival in this country of the new Professor, and the apparatus procured by him for the use of the college."—*The Character of Rush,* by Thomas D. Mitchell, Prof. in the Philadelphia College of Medicine. Philadelphia, 1848, p. 6.

[17] Dr. Rush in describing his experience as a physician in Philadelphia after his return from the battle fields, throws a striking light upon the lack of patriotism in some prominent sections of Pennsylvania society. He says: "The part I took in the American Revolution, had left prejudices in the minds of the most wealthy citizens against me, for a great majority of them

Princeton, the Brandywine, Germantown, and in the sickness at Valley Forge.[18] For twenty-nine years he was surgeon to the Pennsylvania Hospital, and for three years physician to the port of Philadelphia. He was a founder of the Philadelphia Dispensary, and of the College of Physicians. When the scourge of yellow fever broke out in Philadelphia in 1793 he visited from one hundred to one hundred and twenty patients daily.[19] He was the first to proclaim that yellow fever is not contagious and that the disease is indigenous, and his writings on this subject made him famous throughout the world. He has been called the central figure in the medical world of Philadelphia, and gave a new impetus to the study of medicine in this country. It was probably he more than any other single man who made Philadelphia[20] the center of the study of medicine in the United States.

We can see him yet, this man of elegance and refinement, a master in the realm of letters; with professional practise, during later days, of overwhelming magnitude; in appearance slender but well proportioned, with prominent and finely shaped forehead, dignified features, and

---

had been loyalists in principle and conduct."—*Autobiography,* in the *Memorial of Rush,* 1905, p. 63.

[18] He resigned his post in the army, because he could not prevent frauds on soldiers in relation to hospital stores, and other political abuses.

[19] It is said that he is believed, through his method of treatment, to have saved the lives of six thousand persons.

[20] "He has lived for his country, and in a special degree, citizens of Philadelphia, he has lived for you."—Staughton, *An Eulogium,* p. 13.

"His death created a profound impression throughout the United States."—Wilson, p. 8.

eyes of an expressive blue (Nat. Portr. Gallery, III., Rush, p. 10); standing above middle size, dignified but pleasant in his address; seated in his chair and lecturing continuously to his students.

His first class numbered twenty, his last had risen to the enormous number of four hundred and thirty. Six years ago, Dr. James Wilson of Jefferson Medical College, speaking before the American Medical Association, declared, "To us, who behold him through the vista of one hundred years, he stands, not indeed, the most conspicuous figure of a time brilliant with heroic men and deeds, but great among the greatest, and certainly the most striking and impressive figure of the medical life of America at that period or any period since."

Over twenty-two hundred and fifty students attended his courses during his professorship in the Medical College of Philadelphia. When still in full vigor, in the sixty-ninth year of his life, he was seized with an epidemic typhus, and died after a few days' illness on April 19, 1813. He is buried in Christ Church Yard.[21]

Dr. Rush has given us the earliest, and perhaps the most exact history in the English language, of the Pennsylvania-German nature and character. It was written one hundred and twenty years ago, but was intended for English eyes; and we doubt whether many of even the most cultured of the descendants of those whom it describes had ever heard of it before it was brought to light

[21] "If a tombstone be afforded for my death, I ask no further addition to it, than that 'I was an advocate of principles in medicine.'" This inscription was placed upon the tombstone of Dr. Rush in Christ Churchyard, and in 1863 it was said that the only word still thoroughly legible was the word "addition."—*National Portrait Gallery,* Vol. III. *Memorial of Rush,* 10.

and republished thirty-five years ago in a little volume now very rare, by I. D. Rupp, the local historian of many of the eastern counties of Pennsylvania. There are few works of this character able to endure the test of time, and that come to the modern eye with impressiveness, and without an antiquated flavor.[21a]

The period in which Dr. Rush wrote his account of the Germans was a stirring one for the United States. Pennsylvania had been the first state to adopt the new Federal Constitution, in December, 1787; and the president of the state convention which had adopted it was a German. The next year, 1788, the members of the first Congress were elected, and among those from Pennsylvania were a number of Germans. In January, 1789, George Washington was elected the first President of the United States, and in April he passed through Philadelphia in triumphal procession to assume his office. At the close of this eventful year the seat of the national government, for ten years, was fixed in Philadelphia. Meanwhile, the first Congress, in this same year, had chosen a Pennsylvania-German as its first speaker. The president of the State was Benjamin Franklin; but as he was eighty years of age, many of his duties devolved upon the vice president, who up to the fall of 1788 had been General Peter Muhlenberg, another Pennsylvania-German. And now in 1789 and 1790 there was a great struggle going on in Pennsylvania over the new state constitu-

[21a] "No better characterization of the Pennsylvania-Germans has ever been written than that of Dr. Rush, and his little essay, covering about twenty-five pages, is a classic in its way, certainly an historical document to be treated with due seriousness."—Faust, *The German Element in the United States,* Boston, Houghton Mifflin Company. 1909. I, p. 131.

AN ACCOUNT

OF THE

MANNERS

OF THE

GERMAN INHABITANTS

OF PENNSYLVANIA,

WRITTEN 1789,

BY

BENJAMIN RUSH, M. D.

NOTES ADDED

BY

PROF. I. DANIEL RUPP,

Author, Translator, Member of the Historical Society of Pennsylvania; Hon. Mem. Minnesota His. Soc.; Hon. Mem. His. Soc. of Wisconsin; Cor. Mem. of the N. Eng. His. and Genealogical Soc.; Hon. Mem. Phrenakosmian Soc. Pa. Coll.; Hon. Mem. Moravian His. Soc. of Nazareth; Deigmadedachian Soc. of the Theol. Sem. Gettysburg; Hon. Mem. of the Diagnothian Lit. Soc. Marshall Coll; Cor. Mem. York Co. Cabinet of Nat. Sciences and Lyceum; Mem. of Swatara Lit. Inst.; Ehren Mitglied Des Deutschen Pioniers Verein, Cincinnati, O.

PUBLISHED BY
SAMUEL P. TOWN,
614 CHESTNUT ST.
PHILADELPHIA,
1875.

TITLE PAGE OF RUPP'S REPRINT OF DR. RUSH'S ACCOUNT.

(See footnote 34, on p. 28.)

tion to be formulated to harmonize the state government with the federal plan, in which the Germans took part, and in which Dr. Rush was much interested. It was very natural then that Dr. Rush felt the importance of acquainting the American nation with its German citizenship in this year 1789.

The value of Dr. Rush's observations, and his qualifications as a historian of the Pennsylvania-Germans have, perhaps, not been appreciated to their full extent, and it may not be amiss to point them out.

In the first place Dr. Rush, throughout his life, was among, but not of, the German settlers. Born in the Welsh tract in an English settlement, the proximity of the Germans[22] during his youth, and the fresh results of what he actually saw in his younger days, in the midst of a rural community, enabled him to become acquainted with them in the most unvarnished aspects of their existence. Hence when Dr. Rush speaks of the qualities of the Germans as farmers, we can be assured that his observations are born out of actual experience, and are

[22] We have his testimony as to his familiarity with the German language, combined with what must have been an appreciation of the German religious character. In his diary, during the voyage on his return to America after he, as a young man, had completed his studies in Europe, he says, " My friend Mr. Dysert offered to teach me the German language. For this purpose he put a grammar and German dictionary into my hands. By reading the grammar over I became acquainted with the principles and construction of the language. A German steerage passenger furnished me with a Bible in which I read constantly so that in the course of a few weeks I began to understand what I read with but little aid from a translation or a dictionary."—*Autobiography,* in the *Memorial of Rush,* p. 52.

not of the nature of eulogy. We happen to know that Dr. Rush himself was not a stranger in the harvest field. In recounting the days he spent at Dr. Biddle's school, he says: "All his scholars shared in the labors of harvest and haymaking. I bear on one of my fingers to this day the mark of a severe cut I received in learning to reap."[23]

In the second place Dr. Rush's respect for good family stock and his recognition of the sterling worth of an ancestry and of the value of the character of his own forefathers, though in humble apparel and of humble occupation, would enable him to appreciate the merit of similar characteristics in the primitive Germans. In his letter to John Adams on July 13, 1812, he says: "Had any or all of my ancestors appeared before me, in their homespun or working dresses (for they were all farmers or mechanics), they would probably have looked at one another, and said, 'What means that gentleman by thus intruding upon us?' Dear and venerable friends! be not offended at me. I inherit your blood, and I bear the name of most of you. I came here to claim affinity with you, and to do homage to your Christian and moral virtues. It is true, my dress indicates that I move in a different sphere from that in which you have passed through life; but I have acquired and received nothing from the world which I prize so highly as the religious principles which I inherited from you, and I possess nothing that I value so much as the innocence and purity of your characters."

On this letter, Viator, writing on July 4, 1832, makes the following comment: "There is a piety in it—an ardor of feeling and an attachment for the long buried

---

[23] *Autobiography,* in the *Memorial of Rush,* p. 14.

dead—a clinging to the trees that had been planted by the hands long moulded into dust—and an enthusiasm, though stilled by the holiness of the object, which testify the genuineness of the heart's feelings, and give character to him who cherished them. . . . No wonder Rush is immortal. A man that gives proof of such a heart as his can never die."[23a]

In the third place it must not be forgotten that Dr. Rush's observations on the Germans are of unusual value because they were those of a cultured eye witness, who thoroughly knew the people at a sufficiently early date, to enable him to say exactly what they were in their original condition. Dr. Rush was born only three years after Rev. Henry Melchior Muhlenberg first set his foot on American soil, and during the French and Indian War he was an active lad of from twelve to sixteen years of age. He was therefore still in time to have a personal knowledge of the nature and habits of the original immigrants, and also to be able to observe how those same qualities were transformed in the first and second generations of American-born descendants, with the bulk of whom he was a contemporary. The value of such contemporary witness, from the pen of a cultured English writer, cannot be overestimated.

In the fourth place, his life as a medical student in Europe, both in Paris and also in Scotland, gave a setting and a horizon to his estimates of human nature which eliminated all merely local perspectives, and which would be more than ordinarily just and true in reflecting any field of human nature upon which his attention was focused.

In the fifth place the active period of his professional life and work covered the time when Philadelphia, where

[23a] *Autobiography of Rush,* Biddle, pp. 5, 6.

he lived, was the capital of the United States, and when the stirring scenes of Revolutionary days brought out in heightened contrast with each other the various racial qualities of the descendants of the immigrants to this province of William Penn.

To this must be added the fact that Dr. Rush was in continuous contact, professional and intellectual, with the German population of Philadelphia, which formed so large a proportion of the city's total population in those earlier days, and that just as he had been able to estimate the Germans in his younger days, so he was now having an experience extending over many years with the artisans and the professional men who went to the making up of the German community in Philadelphia.

He was on terms of personal intimacy with Dr. Helmuth, the pastor of the large German Lutheran congregation in Philadelphia, and from allusions in his diary we are able to infer that he probably enjoyed a large practice among the parishioners of this flock. He was particularly intimate with Christopher Ludwick, the German philanthropist whose memoir he has written,[24] and whom we suspect he visited frequently, perhaps as a physician, and whom he may possibly have influenced to some extent to the decision to bequeath his estate for educational purposes. In his memoir of Ludwick he says: "Most of the incidents which are to compose the following memoir, were obtained from Mr. Ludwick, by a person who often visited him in the evening of his life. Such of them as were not obtained from that source, were communicated by his family." In

---

[24] *An Account of the Life and Character of Christopher Ludwick,* late citizen of Philadelphia, and Baker-General of the Army of the United States during the Revolutionary War. By

fact, he was a neighbor of Ludwick's,[24a] and was able to observe his life at close range to such an extent that he could say of Ludwick: "He was much esteemed by all who did business with him, for his integrity and punctuality, and for his disposition to do kind offices. His neighbours treated him with so much respect, that he acquired among them the title of 'The Governor of Laetitia Court.'"[24b]

But the crowning qualification of Dr. Rush, in his testimony on behalf of the Pennsylvania-Germans, is the fact that he was a physician, and that he was therefore accustomed to the investigation of facts as they are,[25] and to

---

Benjamin Rush, M.D. First published in the year 1801. Revised and republished by direction of the Philadelphia Society for the establishment and support of charity schools. To which is added an account of the Origin, Progress, and Present Condition of that Institution. Philadelphia: Printed for the Society by Garden and Thompson. 1831.

[24a] Dr. Rush lived on Front St. near Walnut, and again on Fourth St. opposite Willing's Alley, in the house, formerly, of Chief Justice Shippen.

[24b] Rush, *Life of Christopher Ludwick,* p. 9.

[25] The mind of Prof. Rush was characterized by a manly independence.—Staughton, *An Eulogium,* p. 16.

He is always concerned with the matter in hand rather than with the manner of presenting it.—Wilson, *An Address.*

From the result of his individual experience and observation, he established more principles, and added more facts to the science of medicine than all who preceded him in his native land. *Dr. Lieber edition of the Encyclopedia Americana,* quoted by Mitchell, p. 12.

But the best testimony on this point is the language of Rush himself in his *Eulogy on Cullen:*

He says: "Facts are the morality of medicine; they are the same in all countries and throughout all times."

the placing of them on record in the interests of the truth alone, and without the interweaving of any imaginary,[26] legendary, or emotional elements.[27] There is no class of educated men, as a rule, who are so constantly obliged to disentangle a grain of truth from a whole tissue of falsehood, by a searching catechetical process, as are physicians, in their efforts to get at the exact facts in the case. They perhaps learn to understand human nature at its average more thoroughly than any other professional class. It has been said that the minister sees people on their best side, the lawyer sees them on their worst side, and the doctor sees them as they really are. And we may be very certain, from our knowledge of the method which Dr. Rush pursued in all his investigations,[28] and from the attainments which were characteristic of all his literary work, that what he has recorded in this essay is historical testimony of the highest value.[29]

---

[26] "I have been as little disposed to superstition as most men, and have often exposed the folly of being influenced by dreams, by explaining their cause by obvious physical principles."—*Autobiography*, in the *Memorial of Rush*, p. 60.

[27] His fancy was excursive, but his judgment sedate.—Staughton, *An Eulogium*, p. 19.

In the highest sense a man of affairs and a scholar.—Wilson, *An Address in 1904*.

[28] Dr. Rush translated the aphorisms of Hippocrates from the Greek into his vernacular tongue, in the seventeenth year of his age. From this early exercise he probably derived that talent of investigation, that spirit of inquiry, and those extensive views of the nature and causes of disease, which give value to his writings, and have added important benefits to the science of medicine.—Hasock, *To the Memory of Rush*, p. 26.

[29] His eyes and ears were open to see, hear, and profit by every occurrence.—Ramsay, *An Eulogium*, p. 99.

" 'His name,' says Dr. Thomas Young, 'was familiar to the medical world as the Sydenham of America. His accurate observations and correct discrimination of epidemic diseases well entitled him to this distinction, while in the original energy of his reasoning he far exceeded his prototype.'[30] He was a member of nearly every medical, literary and benevolent institution in this country, and of many foreign societies. He taught more clearly than any other physician of his day, how to distinguish diseases and their effects.

"Much of his influence and success was due to his method and regularity of life on the Franklin model. During the thirty years that he attended the Pennsylvania Hospital as physician he is said never to have missed his daily visit and never to have been more than ten minutes late. He was a systematic early riser, and his leisure at the end of the day[31] was spent in reading poetry, history, the moral sciences, and the like, with his pen always in his hand."[32]

---

[30] Rush said: " Medicine without principles is an humble art and a degrading occupation."—Ramsay, *An Eulogium,* p. 98.

[31] " While my days were thus employed in business, my evenings were devoted to study. I seldom went to bed before twelve o'clock, and many, many times have I heard the watchman cry three o'clock, before I put out my candle. I recollect when I began to feel languid or sleepy at late or early hours, I used to excite my mind by increasing the heat and blaze of my fire in winter, or by exposing myself a few minutes in a balcony which projected over Water street, from my back parlour in Front street near Walnut, where I resided till the year 1780, after living but a few months in the house in which I first settled."—*Autobiography,* in the *Memorial of Rush,* p. 59.

[32] One of his mottoes was, "*Studium sine calamo somnium.*"

Rush's writings cover an immense range of subjects, including linguistic, physiological, moral, sociological and historical fields. His last work was an elaborate treatise on the "Diseases of the Mind," 1812. He is best known now by the five volumes of "Medical Inquiries and Observations" which he brought out at intervals from 1789 to 1798 (two later editions revised by the author). He became well known in Europe as an author on the epidemic of yellow fever and was elected an honorary member of several foreign societies.[33] His Medical Inquiries and Observations are in five volumes. His "Essays, Literary, Moral and Philosophical by Benj. Rush, M.D., Thomas and Samuel Bradford, 1798, second edition, 1806; Sixteen Introductory Lectures, 1811," treat all the great subjects of his day and are notable for their close observation, mature thought, and sound reasoning. Among them is to be found his Account of the Germans in Pennsylvania.[34]

That Dr. Rush did not lose his interest in the Germans of Pennsylvania is shown by an essay already alluded to first published in 1801 entitled, An Account of the Life and Character of Christopher Ludwick, by Benj. Rush, M.D.

---

[33] For further information, see Eulogy of Hasock, Essays I, New York, 1824. See References in the works of Thacker, Gross, Bowditch on the history of Medicine in America.

For a fuller statement of his medical positions, see Wilson, p. 7.

[34] The text of *The Account* reproduced in this volume is that of the original "Essays"; not that of Rupp's Reprint of 1875, the facsimile of which is reproduced on page 21.

II. The Title, and The Essay.

IN looking at the title of his essay, it is worthy of notice, first of all, that Rush calls it simply "An Account." Without any thought of grandiloquence, he is simply intent upon setting down a record. The title he chose, beyond any other single characteristic, implies exactitude. It reveals to us that the statements which he is making appeared to him as a description of exact facts, into which he has looked, and which he is able to verify. The term "Account," taken from the mercantile world, and involving columns of debits and credits, of receipts and expenditures, and combination of methodical enumeration,[35] assures us, for purposes of testimony, of greater reliability and exactness, when used by

[35] Dr. Rush was an experienced 'accountant,' and used this word advisedly in the title: "I took the exclusive charge of his [Dr. Redman's] *books and accounts."—Autobiography, in the Memorial of Rush,* p. 19.

an honest writer, than would any more formidable term.

When Dr. Rush tells us that he proposes to present to our eye "An Account of the Manners of the German Inhabitants of Pennsylvania," it is to be borne in mind that the word 'Manners,' now rarely in vogue, was weighted with a meaning in the eighteenth century, which has been worn away in our modern day. The motto of the University of Pennsylvania which asserts that "Letters without Manners are Light and Empty" is an illustration in point. In truth, Dr. Rush says scarcely one word of the personal manners and social etiquette of the people of whom he is writing, and, so simple, unaffected, and earnest, and often blunt, were the manners of the German forefathers, that if used in the merely popular sense, to express a high and hereditary social culture, Rush's title would become a parody on the people whom it was intended to praise.

But the word "manners" has a more substantial sense. It comes to us from the Latin word *manus,* the hand, through the Old French verb *manier* which means to handle, to manage, to wield, and refers to activity and conduct in all the more serious affairs of life. Thoreau has said that "It is the vice of manners that they are continually being deserted by the character; they are cast-off clothes or shells, claiming the respect which belonged to the living creature." It is not of these outer shells of character, but of the active character itself, as shown in their views of life, their ways of doing things, their ideas of management, their deeply ingrained and traditional life-customs, their thoughts and feelings of home, God, business, education, and the other great *verities,* of which Dr. Rush wrote an account.

At the close of the eighteenth century, when the life of our commonwealth was new and young, Dr. Rush termed the people whom we call Pennsylvania-Germans, "the German inhabitants of Pennsylvania," for obvious reasons. In referring to the newer states in our great Northwest we still speak of the German, the Scandinavian, and the Danish immigrant. Dr. Rush called the Germans, of whom he was about to give an account, "inhabitants" and not "immigrants," because their life had already reached a fixity. They were integral parts of the community. They were here to stay and constituted a very large part of the colony. But they were still "Germans" either of the first or original, or of the second, and in some cases of the third generation; they were not yet "Pennsylvania-Germans," for this compound term implies a double determining factor in the stock of the people, in which the part that "Pennsylvania" has played is as important in its way as is the original German element.

Dr. Rush might have used the term "citizens," instead of "inhabitants," as giving a more honorable and definite political and national quality to the blood of our German forefathers, but we believe that the term "inhabitants" was chosen because the book is somewhat in the form of a geographical description, rather than of a historical or political treatise; and as a matter of fact, and curiously enough, in the very first sentence of his essay Dr. Rush makes the fullest possible amends for the use, in the title, of the word "inhabitants" by actually calling the people "German citizens," and by ascribing a large part of the prosperity and reputation of the state to their citizenship. He says: "The State of Pennsylvania is so much indebted for her prosperity and reputation to *the German part of her citizens* that a short Account of their Manners may, perhaps, be useful and agreeable *to their fellow-citizens* in every part of the United States." He thus records the Germans in Pennsylvania as being already at that date of an honorable and established citizenship, and worthy of an English treatise, which should draw the favorable attention of "their fellow-citizens in every part of the United States."

The Essay.

In coming to analyze the Essay itself, we notice that it is composed of only about 6,700 words, and the whole production would easily go into eight or nine columns of any of our morning papers. After a brief introduction devoted to the original immigrants, narrating from whence in Germany, and under what situation, they came to America; and taking pains to describe to us, that, though they brought little property, they had, in addition to a few pieces of silver or gold and a chest with clothes, "a Bible and Prayer or Hymn Book;" that they paid for their own passage across the sea, many after the manner of the redemptioner; and that *"a clergyman always accompanied* them when they came in large bodies;"[36] he tells of their occupations and trades.

He then proceeds to dwell at length upon the German farmers, and presents no less than sixteen characteristics in numerical order, prefacing these characteristics with a brief eulogy on their industry, frugality, and skill, and with the declaration that the farm of a German could be distin-

---

[36] One of his biographers informs us that throughout the extensive practice of a life time Dr. Rush never shut out a clergyman from the visitation of a sick patient.

"It was well known in Philadelphia that Dr. Rush more frequently attended public worship, than, perhaps any other physician."—Mitchell, p. 18.

guished from that of other settlers in Pennsylvania "by good fences, the extent of orchards, the fertility of the soil, the productiveness of the fields, the luxuriance of the meadows."

The first of the agricultural points enumerated by Dr. Rush, relates to the management and to the buildings of the Germans, the second to their ability to choose good land and to their enhancement of its value, the third to their thorough clearing of the land. "They do not girdle or belt the trees simply or leave them to perish in the ground as is the custom of their English or Irish neighbors." He speaks in the fourth place of their good feeding of cattle, in the fifth place of their well-built fences, in the sixth place of their conservation of natural resources, a vital fact to which the American nation is only now, a century and a half later, beginning to awake, as a nation. He thinks of the fact also that despite their economy, "their houses are rendered so comfortable at all times . . . that twice the business is done by every branch of the family as that is done in houses where every member of the family crowds near a common fire place or shivers at a distance from it."

He notes in the seventh place the care and attention given to their live-stock. In the eighth place he speaks of their personal household habits and their food. While he mentions that it has been thought, by reason of their sparing use of animal food, "that they decline in strength sooner than their English or Irish neighbors," he goes on to say that "very few of them used distilled spirits in their families." He approves of their use of light feather beds instead of blankets, and he refers to the home-spun apparel of the farmers, adding, "When they use European articles of dress, they prefer those of the best quality and of the highest prices. They are afraid of debt and seldom purchase anything without paying cash for it." In the ninth place, Dr. Rush refers to the large gardens of the Pennsylvania Germans, and he goes so far as to say that "Pennsylvania is indebted to the Germans for *the principal part of her knowledge in horticulture.*"

He notes in the tenth place that the work on the farms is done by members of the family rather than by servants; that the travel is by large strong wagons; and, in the twelfth place that the German inhabitants love and rejoice in many children. "Happy state of human society!" exclaims he. "The joy of parents upon the birth of a child is the grateful echo of creating goodness!" exclaims he. "May the mountains of Pennsylvania be forever filled with songs of joy upon these occasions!" exclaims he. And he adds, "They will be the infallible signs of industry, wealth and happiness in the State."

In the thirteenth place Dr. Rush points to the fact that the Germans in Pennsylvania (exemplifying what was to be John Ruskin's strong Saxon ideal of work and labor[37]),

---

[37] Ruskin says, "To succeed to my own satisfaction in a manual piece of work, is life, to me, as to all men."—*Fors,* II., p. 306.

"The beginning of all good law, and nearly the end of it, is in these two ordinances: That every man shall do good work for his bread; and secondly, That every man shall have good bread for his work."—*Fors,* I., p. 141.

"A happy nation may be defined as one in which the husband's hand is on the plough, and the housewife's on the needle; so in due time reaping its golden harvest, and shining in golden vesture: and an unhappy nation is one which, acknowledging no use of plough nor needle, will assuredly at last find its storehouse empty in the famine, and its breast naked to the cold."—*The Two Paths,* p. 121.

take great pains to train their children not merely *in habits* of labor, but *into a love* of it. "They instil a fear of God[38] and a love of work." Says he, "They prefer industrious habits to money itself."

In the fourteenth place Dr. Rush draws attention approvingly to the value the Germans set upon patrimony. In the fifteenth place he speaks of their superstition in planting trees in accordance with the appearance of the moon, and intimates that the influence of the moon upon the earth may after all be a scientific fact rather than a superstition. In the sixteenth place, he tells us that plenty and neatness in everything that "belonged to them" distinguished the German farms "from the farms of the other citizens of the State."

Passing now from the German farmer to the mechanic, he emphasizes first of all the desire of every German mechanic to become a freeholder, and secondly the German mechanic's knowledge of both the European and the newer and more distinctively American mechanical arts.

Of the merchants, he shows that they are candid and punctual, and makes the following statement, "The Bank of North America has witnessed from its first institution their fidelity to all their pecuniary engagements." These are the words of a man who was Treasurer of the United States Mint to the day of his death.

After describing their agricultural and mechanical life,

---

[38] In the letter to John Adams, late President of the United States, the original of which was in the hand of Dr. Hasock, Dr. Rush wrote concerning his parents: "I have acquired and received nothing from the world which I prize so highly as the religious principles I inherited from them; and I possess nothing that I value so much as the innocence and purity of their characters."—Hasock, *To the Memory of Rush,* p. 24.

Dr. Rush proceeds to give the result of his observations on their religious, educational, political, social, and ecclesiastical life; and as to their value, as an asset, to the commonwealth of Pennsylvania. Perhaps the most remarkable of all the statements that he makes in this essay, and the tribute than which no greater could be paid to any people, is the one in which he connects their good character and citizenship in later life, directly with their earlier religious and educational training. He says: "All the different sects among them are particularly attentive to the religious education of their children, and to the establishment and support of the Christian Religion. For this purpose they settle as much as possible, together, and make the erection of a school-house, and a place of worship, the first object of their care. They commit the education and instruction of their children, in a peculiar manner, to the ministers and officers of their churches; hence they grow up with *biases* in favor of public worship, and of the obligations of Christianity. Such has been the influence of a pious education among the *Germans,* in Pennsylvania, that in the course of nineteen years, only *one* of them, has ever been brought to a place of public shame or punishment."

Writers of English blood, from Benjamin Franklin down to John Fiske, and others in Pennsylvania, who, whether from prejudice or because they have accepted the vulgar traditions afloat in American literature, as to the low character and the ignorance of a people which the English immigrants did not understand,[38a] would have to go very far among their own people to match a record such as this.

[38a] The English people has always been dull and slow in its comprehension of the German genius and character. "English authors did not discover Germany until 1780, and not until William

Of their political life, Dr. Rush says they are peaceable, prompt in payment of taxes, and loyal. In their social life he emphasizes their hospitality as genuine and free from avariciousness, their willingness to lend money to those who prove themselves to be trustworthy, and their excellence in vocal and instrumental music.

That Dr. Rush has not closed his eyes to the limited culture of the German forefathers, is to be seen from his remarks as to their superstitions, their ignorance of the forms of English law, and their trust in quack doctors; but he also testifies to their thoughtfulness and intelligence in their own language since they maintain a large number of German newspapers circulated throughout the state; and he says definitely, "There is scarcely an instance of a German of either sex in Pennsylvania that cannot *read;* but many of the wives and daughters of the German farmers cannot *write.*"[39] He speaks with approval of the learned sons of the Germans, rising in his generation, and of the new German college in Pennsylvania.[40]

After devoting a large part of his essay to explaining the ecclesiastical and social peculiarities of the German

---

Taylor had translated many German literary works, and the poets, Wordsworth, Coleridge, Walter Scott, and subsequently Thomas Carlyle, beat a trail into the 'kingdom of the mind.'"—Faust, *The German Element in the United States,* II., p. 209.

[39] As a whole they were not opposed to education . . . and established schools from the earliest date. Michael Schlatter and Henry Melchior Muhlenberg, the leaders of the Reformed and Lutheran Germans, were in favor of the higher education.—Barr Ferree, *Pennsylvania: A Primer,* 1904.

[40] Franklin and Marshall College at Lancaster, Pa. Dr. Rush was greatly interested in the founding of Dickinson College at Carlisle, Pa.

bodies settled in the state, he again reverts to the value of the Germans as citizens of this commonwealth, and to the results of a single generation of their toil in the midst of freedom: "If it were possible to determine the amount of all the property brought into Pennsylvania, by the present German inhabitants of the state, and their ancestors, and then compare it with the present amount of their property, the contrast would form such a monument of human industry and economy, as has seldom been contemplated in any age or country."

Reminding his readers of the strength of the early Germanic character as portrayed on the pages of ancient history, our author closes this remarkable essay by pointing out what the whole country in his own day might learn from the German in Pennsylvania.

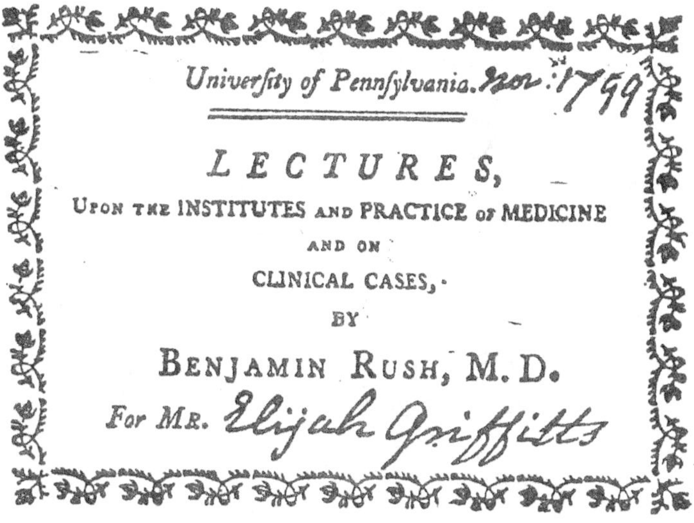

University of Pennsylvania. Nov: 1799

LECTURES,

UPON THE INSTITUTES AND PRACTICE OF MEDICINE

AND ON

CLINICAL CASES,

BY

BENJAMIN RUSH, M.D.

For MR. Elijah Griffitts

AN ACCOUNT OF THE MANNERS OF THE GERMAN INHABITANTS OF PENNSYLVANIA.

THE State of Pennsylvania[1] is so much indebted

---

[1] Pennsylvania was discovered by the Swedes and the Dutch, owned by the English, and preferred as a paradise for migration by the Germans. The Germans hastened hither from New York, which bitter experience had taught them to shun, and from the Fatherland.

" Not satisfied with being themselves removed from New York, they wrote to their friends and relatives, if ever they intended to come to America, not to go to New York. This advice had such influence that the Germans, who afterwards went in such numbers to America, constantly avoided New York and went to Pennsylvania. It sometimes happened that they were forced to take ships bound for New York, but they were scarce got on shore when they hastened to Pennsylvania, *in sight of all the in-*

for her prosperity[2] and reputation,[3] to the German part[4] of her citizens, that a short account of their

---

habitants of New York."—Peter Kalm, the Swedish naturalist and traveler, v. *Penn. Hist. Mag.*, X., 388.

"We are daily expecting ships from London, which bring over Palatines, in number about six or seven thousand. We had a parcel who came out about five years ago, and proved quiet and industrious."—James Logan.

[2] Pennsylvania took the lead of all the colonial states in agriculture, because of the many German settlers. In 1751, there were exported 86,000 bushels of wheat, 129,960 barrels of flour, 90,743 bushels of Indian corn. The total exports of 1751, exceeded in value, one million of dollars.—I. D. Rupp.

Lieutenant Governor George Thomas, in 1738, while addressing the Council on some action proposed in restriction of immigration declared: "This Province has been for some years the asylum of the distressed Protestants of the Palatinate and other parts of Germany, and I believe it may with truth be said, that the present flourishing condition of it is in a great measure owing to the industry of those people; and should any discouragement divert them from coming hither, it may well be apprehended that the value of your lands will fall, and your advance to wealth be much slower."—*Penn. Col. Records,* III., 315.

[3] The reputation of the German element in Pennsylvania for industry, thrift and piety caused Mortimer, *History of England,* III., 233, to write: "Pennsylvania is since become by far the most populous and flourishing colony for its standing of any in British America."

[4] THE GERMAN POPULATION OF THE PROVINCE.

The German part of Pennsylvania was its large part. Barr Ferree, *Primer of Pennsylvania,* p. 92, says that the Germans "formed a large proportion of the population of Pennsylvania,

manners[5] may, perhaps, be useful and agreeable to their fellow citizens in every part of the United States.

---

estimated at from one-half to one-third in the provincial period." Governor Thomas estimated the Germans as constituting about three-fifths of the population. We may say that there were 20,000 Germans in Pennsylvania before 1727, the year in which migration became extensive. To these we may add 18,000 more up to 1742. By the end of 1748, 6,000 more had arrived. Between 1749 and 1754 nearly 32,000 arrived through the port of Philadelphia. Nine or ten thousand more arrived through the same port prior to the Revolution. In 1759 Dr. William Smith tells the Archbishop of Canterbury that a little more than one-fifth of the 250,000 souls in Pennsylvania are Germans. This is too low an estimate and it is commonly supposed that the Germans, prior to the Revolutionary War, constituted at least one-third of the entire population. Such is Benjamin Franklin's estimate, who in 1776 testified before a committee of the British House of Commons that of the 160,000 whites in the Province of Pennsylvania about one-third were Germans.

In this testimony Franklin described the Germans as "a people who brought with them the greatest of all wealth,—industry and integrity and character that had been superpoised and developed by years of suffering and persecution."—*Penn. Hist. Mag.*, IV., 3.

The *Hallesche Nachrichten,* I., 411, makes possible an estimate of Lutheran and Reformed in Pennsylvania at ninety thousand in 1748. Kuhns estimates the number of Germans in Pennsylvania in 1775 as nearly ninety thousand, and adds twenty thousand for the natural increase. Faust also places the number of Germans and German descendants in 1775 at one hundred and ten thousand, and in 1790 at sixty thousand. See Schmauk, *The Lutheran Church in Pennsylvania,* p. 28; Faust, *The German Element in the United States,* I., 128, 282; II., 12–27.

[5] See Introduction, for a discussion of Dr. Rush's use of this term.

The aged Germans,[6] and the ancestors of those who are young, migrated[7] chiefly from the Palatinate;[8] from Alsace,[9] Swabia,[10] Saxony,[11] and

---

[6] The original immigrants.

[7] See *The German Emigration to America, 1709–1740*, by Henry Eyster Jacobs, *Proceedings of the Pennsylvania-German Society*, Vol. VIII. Also, *The Emigration from New York Province into Pennsylvania*, by Mathias Henry Richards, *Proceedings of Pennsylvania-German Society*, Vol. IX.

[8] The Pilgrim Fathers were not the only company who sought in this western world "Freedom to worship God." The fact is that, if ever a body of emigrants came to America from under the hand of the oppressor, such were these Palatines; and if ever the thought of religious liberty constrained men to leave their native land for hoped-for freedom in America, such hope was powerful with these children of the Palatinate. Hence it is, that the story of their coming hither, with the bitterness and pathos of their antecedent suffering and endurance, and the sturdiness of their unconquerable faith and determination to wrest fortune and happiness out of the very talons of despair, is one that should be better known to the student of American history.—Cobb, *The Story of the Palatines*, pp. 12, 13.

For the history of this great deportation, see Diffenderffer, "*The German Emigration into Pennsylvania through the Port of Philadelphia,*" *Proceedings of the Pennsylvania-German Society*, Vol. X.

[9] A good sprinkling of settlers from Alsace were found early in parts of Berks and Lehigh Counties, many of them with names originally French.

[10] The Wuertembergers came over later than the Palatines, in large and steady influx.

[11] See Pennypacker, *Crefeld*, *Proceedings of the Pennsylvania-German Society*, Vol. IX.

Switzerland;[12] but natives of every principality and dukedom of Germany[13] are to be found[14] in different parts of the state. They brought[15] but little property[16] with them. A few pieces of

---

[12] See Rupp, *Swiss Immigrants in Pennsylvania, 1727–1776.* Harrisburg, 1856, 2d ed., Phila., 1876; Kuhns, *The German and Swiss Settlements of Colonial Pennsylvania;* Gibbons, *Swiss Exiles.*

[13] See Sachse, *The Fatherland: Showing the Part it Bore in the Discovery, Exploration and Development of the Western Continent with special reference to the Commonwealth of Pennsylvania, Proceedings of the Pennsylvania-German Society,* Vol. VII.

[14] See Rupp, *Thirty Thousand Names.*

In the ship lists, the name Palatines is indiscriminately applied to all imported Germans into Pennsylvania, prior to 1741; afterwards, they are designated foreigners, inhabitants of the Palatinate, and places adjacent; Wittembergers, from Erbach, foreigners from Wittemberg, Alsace, and Zweibruecken: from Nassau, Hanau, Darmstadt, Alsatians, Eisenberg, Basal, Swabia, Mannheim, Durlach, Rittenheim: inhabitants of Lorraine, Mentz, Franconia, Hesse, Hamburg, Saxony. After 1754, principalities, the dukedoms, districts, places or towns, are not designated in the ship lists.—I. D. Rupp.

[15] See Gottlieb Mittelberger, *Reise nach Pennsylvanien,* im Jahr 1750. Frankfuhrt und Leipzig, 1756.

[16] Many who at home had owned property, and converted it into money, were robbed in transitu, by ship owners, importers, sea captains, and *Neulaender.* The emigrants' chests, with their clothes, and sometimes their money, were put on other vessels or ships, and left behind. These chests were rifled of their contents. The German immigrants thus treated, on their arrival at Philadelphia, were obliged to submit to being sold as *Loskaeuflinge, Redemptioners,* they and their children, to pay their passage money. In not a few cases, persons, who still had means, were

gold or silver coin,[17] a chest filled with clothes, a bible, and a prayer or an hymn book[18] constituted

---

held responsible to pay the passage for the poorer. This was the practice for more than fifty years. In this way, persons of substance were necessitated, and did become, very frequently, common beggars. *Col. Rec.*, IV., 586; *Penna. Arch.*, IV., 472; *Gordon's History of Penna.*, p. 300.—I. D. Rupp.

[17] These pieces of coin were often kept for many years, against the last emergency, and, at times, were highly prized as family pieces because of their history. Dr. Rush himself, in his *Life of Christopher Ludwick*, p. 28, alludes to a coin of this kind. He says: " In every stage and situation of life, Mr. Ludwick appeared to be, more or less, under the influence of the doctrines and precepts of Christianity. Part of this influence, it has been said, was derived from his education. . . . His father inherited a piece of silver of the size of a French crown, . . . with the following words in its exergue, ' The blood of Christ cleanseth from all sin.' I John 1: 7. . . . This piece of silver Mr. Ludwick carried in his pocket, in all his voyages and travels in Europe, Asia and America. It was closely associated in his mind, with the respect and affection he bore for his ancestors, and with a belief of his interest in the blessings of the Gospel. In looking at it in all his difficulties and dangers, he found animation and courage. In order to insure its safety . . . he had it fixed . . . in the lid of a silver tankard, . . . and under it the following motto: ' May the religion, industry and courage of a German parent, be the inheritance of his issue.' "

[18] Books of the Pennsylvania Germans.

They brought with them copies of *the Bible, hymn-book, prayer-book, catechism, sermon-book* and other devotional books. Court Chaplain Boehm, of London, rendered an important service to immigrants sent from England to America by securing for them copies of Arndt's *Wahres Christenthum.* Starke's *Gebet Buch* was also used by many settlers. . . . Religious

the whole stock of most of them. Many of them bound[19] themselves, or one or more of their chil-

books were imported from the Fatherland. . . . German religious books were published in this country at a very early day. In 1708 Justus Falkner published the first book of a Lutheran minister printed in America. . . . In 1728 appeared *Das Büchlein vom Sabbath,* and *Neun und neunzig mystische Sprüche,* by Conrad Beissel. *Hymn-books* were printed in 1730, 1732, 1739, 1742, and the Bible in 1743, Luther's *Catechism* annotated by Zinzendorf in 1744, *the New Testament* in 1745, *the Psalter* in 1746, the *Martyrer-Spiegel* in 1748, Arndt's *Wahres Christenthum* in 1751, etc.—Schantz, *Domestic Piety and Religion, Proceedings of the Pennsylvania-German Society,* X., pp. 39–50.

On May 9, 1753, Benjamin Franklin said of the Germans: "They import many books from Germany, and of the six printing houses in the Province, two are entirely German, two half German and half English, and two are entirely English."—Sparks, *Works of Franklin,* VII., p. 71.

The Dunkers in Germany raised by subscription a sum of money to purchase religious books and disperse them among their poor friends in Pennsylvania, and sent over the printing press afterward used so effectively by Christopher Saur.

For the extensive publication enterprises of the Germans in Pennsylvania, see, Seidensticker, *The First Century of German Printing in America,* also Hildebrand, and supplementary information by Stapleton, and others.

[19] Prior to 1727, most of the Germans came in companies, or were persons of means. "In the years 1728, '29, '37, '41, '50 and '51, large numbers of Redemptioners, or those who bound themselves, came to Pennsylvania."—Loeher, p. 80.

The usual terms of sale depended somewhat on the age, strength and health of the persons sold. Boys and girls usually had to serve from five to ten years, till they attained the age of twenty-one. Many parents were necessitated, as they had been wont at

dren, to masters after their arrival, for four, five, or seven years, in order to pay for their passages across the ocean.[20] A clergyman[21] always accompanied them when they came in large bodies.

---

home to do with their cattle, to *sell their own children.* The children had to assume the passage money, both their own, and that of their parents, in order that the latter might be released from the ship. Children under five years of age could not be sold. They were disposed of gratuitously to such persons as agreed to raise them, and let them go free when they attained the age of twenty-one.

It was an humble position that Redemptioners occupied. "Yet," says Gordon, "from this class have sprung some of the most reputable and wealthy inhabitants of this province."—Gordon, *His. Pa.*, p. 556.—I. D. Rupp.

For an extensive description of the *Neulaènder* and the arrival of the Redemptioners, together with the work of the German Society in Philadelphia, see note in *Hallesche Nachrichten,* II., pp. 459–461, 709. See also, I., pp. 273, 515, 675, 700.

For material concerning the Redemptioners see Mittelberger, *Reise nach Pennsylvanien;* Rupp, *Thirty Thousand Names;* Diffenderffer, *The Redemptioners, Proceedings of Pennsylvania-German Society,* X., 5–315; *Record of Individuals Bound out as Apprentices, Servants, etc., and of the German and other Redemptioners in the Office of the Mayor in Philadelphia, October 3, 1771, to October 5, 1773, Proceedings of the Pennsylvania-German Society,* XVI., pp. 1–325; Faust, *The German Element in the United States,* pp. 66–72.

[20] The journey across the ocean was a serious affair; and frequently undertaken under the spiritual guidance of the pastor. Thus the pioneer pastor Joshua Kocherthal, with the first of the Palatines, left his home at Landau in Germany with sixty-one persons, scarcely knowing whither to go, came to London in the spring of 1708, and sent a memorial to the Queen on behalf of

his "poor Lutherans, come hither from the lower Palatinate praying to be transferred to some of your Majesty's plantations in America; in number forty-one . . . being reduced to this miserable condition by the ravages committed by the French when they lost all they had."

Kocherthal again came over at the head of the emigration of 1710, and as pastor of the immigrants in all the Hudson settlements exercised the greatest influence, together with John Fred. Hager, of the Reformed faith, at whose marriage Kocherthal officiated.

When Muhlenberg, a generation later, crossed the sea to Charleston, in a voyage of 110 days on an emigrant vessel, we read that "the ship became a church, his fellow-passengers, the crew and several negro slaves, a mission field for this ambassador of the Cross. Although suffering exceedingly from sea sickness he is seen daily instructing in intellectual and spiritual things the children on board. Sunday after Sunday he preaches, in the morning German to the few Salzburgers on board, in the afternoon with blundering attempts at an English discourse, using Latin terms where his limited vocabulary failed him and having the captain put them into English. Every one was taken under his pastoral supervision. To the negroes especially he gave the kindliest attention, endeavoring to plant in them the germs of religious knowledge. Excepting the few Salzburgers there was not one on board who could enter into his religious views and feelings or even afford him social companionship, yet he commanded by his Christian demeanor and official faithfulness the high personal esteem of the whole ship's company."—Wolf, pp. 244–245.

[21] THE EARLY GERMAN CLERGYMEN IN THE PROVINCE.

The first clergymen to arrive in Pennsylvania were the Swedish pastors, the Rev. Reorus Torkillus in 1639; and the Rev. John Campanius, the translator of Luther's Catechism into English, antedating in actual use the Indian Bible of John Elliot, and who held services on Sundays and festival days, preached on Wednesdays and Fridays, and conducted daily matins and vespers at Tinicum, nine miles southwest of Philadelphia, in 1646. The first German preacher in Pennsylvania was the Lutheran Jacobus Fabritius in 1671. Then came the settlers of Germantown, under Pastorius, their spiritual leader. A letter from Germantown, dated Feb. 12, 1684, probably written by Hermans Op den Graeff, says "One finds in Pennsylvania (excluding ourselves) Lutheran and Reformed. The former have two ministers. Their fruits, however, give testimony that they are teachers without the Spirit. At New Castle mostly Hollanders reside. The Reformed have no minister here at present. The Papists here hold no meetings." The chaplain of the band of Pietists, Henrich Bernard Köster, arrived in 1694, and held the first German Lutheran services in Germantown, and the first English services in Philadelphia. Then came the Mennonites, who were very religious. From 1700 and 1701, the Falckner brothers attempted to provide for the spiritual condition of the Lutherans in Pennsylvania, and in 1703 Justus Falckner became the first minister ordained in this Country. In 1710 the Dutch Reformed pastor, Paulus Van Vlecq, organized the White Marsh Church at Neshaminy. In the same year Samuel Guldin, a minister of the Reformed Church in Switzerland reached Pennsylvania. In 1717 the Rev. Gerhart Henkel arrived at Falckner Swamp and went forth as a circuit preacher into distant parts of the wilderness in southeastern Pennsylvania. In 1725 John Philip Boehm began his useful labors among the Reformed immigrants.

In September, 1727, the Rev. George Michael Weis came to Philadelphia with a company of about four hundred emigrants from the Palatinate; and, in September, 1728, the greatest of the pioneer pastors and organizer of churches, the Rev. John Caspar Stoever, arrived. At the same time the Rev. John Peter Miller, a most learned man, and subsequently identified with the Ephrata community, and Conrad Beissel still earlier, were active in the regions of the Tulpehocken. Meantime the Moravian missionaries arrived, and a little over a decade later, Count Zinzendorf

The principal part of them were farmers;[22] but there were many mechanics, who brought with them a knowledge of those arts[23] which are neces-

himself appeared in America. In 1742 Henry Melchior Muhlenberg, the founder and organizer, arrived in America, the first of the long line of ministers sent out by Francke and the Halle Orphan House, to supply the immigrants in this country; and in 1746 Michael Schlatter arrived and occupied a similar position amid the Reformed emigrants. These clergymen were all learned men, and many of them university graduates.

[22] "The Germans seem more adapted to agriculture and improvement of a wilderness; and the Irish, for trade. The Germans soon get estates in this country, where industry and economy are the chief requisites to procure them." *Proud's His. of Pa.,* II., 274. On this whole paragraph relating to agricultural and mechanical arts, see Schantz, *Domestic Life and Characteristics of the Pennsylvania-German Pioneer, Proceedings of the Pennsylvania-German Society,* X, p. 5. See also forthcoming paper by Albert Rau, *Some Notes on Trades as Found among the Germans of Pennsylvania.*

[23] At the close of the term of apprenticeship, the young mechanic, before he was allowed to set up for himself, was obliged, according to the custom of Guilds and Trades, in Germany, to make his *Wanderschaft, Peregrination,* of one or more years, in order to perfect himself in his trade; and, he had to show some well finished piece of workmanship, before he could be promoted to the honor of master-workman, in any town, except where he was raised.

The *Wanderschaft* custom, if properly improved, afforded opportunities to acquire, besides a proficiency in their trade, much useful knowledge in general, which books alone could not supply. For the intention of this custom, was, that the *Handwerks-Bursch* (Travelling Journeyman) should gain experience in his craft, and learn methods practised in the countries, besides his own, as well as some knowledge of the world. It is nothing

sary and useful in all countries. These mechanics[24]

---

unusual to meet, in Germany, with common mechanics, who speak three or four different languages, well informed as to the state of most of the countries of Europe, and possessing a general fund of knowledge, far superior to what is found in persons of the same class, in England. Murray, *Handbook,* p. 218, quoted by I. D. Rupp.

[24] Francis Daniel Pastorius, founder of Germantown, in a German letter written to Germany from Philadelphia as early as March 7, 1684, presents the following interesting picture of his company of immigrants to America: "Our company was made up of many kinds of people; there was a doctor of medicine, with his wife and eight children, a French captain, a Low Dutch cake-baker, an apothecary, a glass-blower, mason, smith, wheelwright, cabinetmaker, cooper, hatter, cobbler, tailor, gardener, husbandmen, seamstresses, etc., in all and sundry, eighty persons, besides the ship's crew. These differed not only in their ages (our oldest woman was 60 years old, while the youngest child was but twelve weeks old) and in their occupations just mentioned, but they were also of such different religions and ways of living, that I might not improperly compare the ship that brings them hither to the Ark of Noah, unless more unclean than clean (rational) beasts are contained therein. Among my domestics I have such as hold with Roman, the Lutheran, the Calvinistic, the Anabaptist and the Church of England, but only one Quaker." —Sachse, *Letters Relating to the Settlement of Germantown,* p. 11.

From the middle of April, 1709, to the middle of July, 1709, there arrived at London, 11,294 German Protestants—males and females. Male occupations: husbandmen and vine dressers, 1,838; bakers, 56; masons, 87; carpenters, 124; shoemakers, 68; tailors, 99; butchers, 29; millers, 45; tanners, 14; stocking weavers, 7; barbers, 6; locksmiths, 4; cloth and linen weavers, 95; coopers, 82; hunters, 7; saddlers, 13; glassblowers, 2; hatters, 3; lime-

were chiefly weavers, taylors, tanners, shoemakers, comb-makers, smiths of all kinds, butchers, paper-makers, watch makers, and sugar bakers.[25] I shall begin this account of the German inhabitants of Pennsylvania, by describing the manners of the German farmers.

This body of citizens are not only industrious[26] and frugal,[27] but skilful cultivators of the earth.

---

burners, 8; schoolmasters, 18; engravers, 2; bakers, 22; brick-makers, 3; silversmiths, 2; smiths, 35; herdsmen, 3; blacksmiths, 48; potters, 3; turners, 6; silversmiths, 2; statuary, 1; surgeons, 2; masons, 39. Of the 11,294 emigrants, 2,556 had families.—Kapp, pp. 89, 90; *Frankfurter-Mess-Kalendar von Ostern bis Herbst,* 1709, pp. 90.—I. D. Rupp.

[25] In speaking of the sugar bakers it is quite possible that Dr. Rush had his friend Christopher Ludwick, the "Baker-General of the Army of the United States during the Revolutionary War," in mind. Though a mere craftsman, his early education in Germany is typical of the training these emigrants received. Dr. Rush says of him: "At fourteen years of age he was sent to a free school, where he was taught to read and write, and the common rules of arithmetic. He was carefully instructed at the same time, in the principles of the Christian religion as held by the Lutherans. Of this school he always retained a grateful remembrance."—Rush, *Life of Christopher Ludwick,* pp. 6, 7.

More than fifty persons had been taught reading, writing and arithmetic at his expense, in different schools in the city and its neighborhood. The principal part of his business for many years before he died, was to find out and relieve objects of distress.—Rush, *Life of Christopher Ludwick,* p. 22.

[26] For a picture of their industry, see W. J. Mann, *"Die Gute Alte Zeit" in Pennsylvanien,* Phila., Kohler, 1880.

[27] For an explanation and defense of this frugality, see Dr. George Mays, *The Early Pennsylvania-German Farmer, The*

I shall enumerate a few particulars, in which they differ[28] from most of the other farmers of Pennsylvania.

Pennsylvania-German, October, 1901, pp. 186–188. Among other things, Dr. Mays says: "One of the strongest arguments in favor of their generosity and helpfulness is found in the fact that the squalor and poverty, so frequently seen in the midst of the great wealth and boasted charities of our large cities, are, and always have been, entirely unknown in the farming communities of the Pennsylvania-Germans."

[28] The *German's* farm was easily distinguished from those of others, by good fences, the extent of orchard, the fertility of soil, productiveness of the fields, the luxuriance of the meadows. *Colum-Mag.* for 1790.—I. D. Rupp.

The Farmers.

1st. In settling a tract of land,[29] they always provide large and suitable accommodations for their horses and cattle, before they lay out much money in building a house for themselves. The barn[30] and stables are generally under one roof, and contrived in such manner as to enable them to feed their horses and cattle, and to remove their dung, with as little trouble as

---

[29] As to the taking up of land by the settlers and acquiring of tracts, consult the manuscript *Surveys and Land Warrants*, found among "Taylor's *Papers,* Being a Collection of Warrants, Surveys, Letters, etc., Relating to the Early Settlements of Pennsylvania." Jacob Taylor was Surveyor General of Pennsylvania from 1701–1733.

[30] Later, (16th), Dr. Rush again refers to the more fully developed Pennsylvania-German barn.

"And what barns! No community on earth can boast of finer and larger barns than these 'Switzers' of our Lebanon Valley Pennsylvania-German Georgic princes. Yet such is the skill of this king of farmers, this Pennsylvania-German, that even

possible. The first dwelling house[31] upon this farm[32] is small, and built of logs. It generally

---

these gigantic store houses are often known to overflow with farm products and rows of hive-shaped stacks of hay and grain have to be set near by as so many sentinels to guard the rich farm treasures."—Croll, *Ancient and Historic Landmarks in the Lebanon Valley*, p. 17.

[31] The first home was the original log cabin in the wilderness, without foundations. This gave way to substantial log buildings, "of the dimensions of fifteen feet square at the least," with a masonry foundation and "a good chimney of brick or stone to be laid in and built with lime and sand."—Schmauk, *Old Salem in Lebanon*, pp. 41, 48.

The first log house was a very plain construction. Its sides were of logs; the openings between the logs were filled with clay, often mixed with grass. Windows were of small dimensions. Doors were often of two parts, an upper and a lower, hung or fastened separately. The interior was frequently only one room, with hearth and chimney, with a floor of stone or hardened clay, with steps or a ladder leading to the attic, with roughly constructed tables and benches, plainly made bedsteads, shelving on the walls and wooden pegs driven into the logs. The pioneer's house was not complete without the large fireplace, often in the center of the buildings and very often on one of the sides of the house, with hearth and chimney erected outside of the building, yet joining the same.—Schantz, *The Pennsylvania-German as Pioneer and Home Builder, Proceedings of the Pennsylvania-German Society*, X. The article goes on to describe the contents and various rooms of the house at length.

[32] A house built by a German, could, even at a distance, be readily distinguished from one erected by a Scotch, Irish or Englishman. Had the house but one chimney, and this in the middle (*in der Mitte des Hauses*), then it was a German's. They had stoves. To economize in the use of stove pipes, the

lasts the life time of the first settler of a tract of land; and hence they have a saying, that "a son should always begin his improvements where his father left off,"—that is, by building a large and convenient stone house.[33]

2d. They always prefer good land[34] or that land on which there is a large quantity of meadow

---

chimney occupied the central portion. A house with a chimney at each gable end, was erected by an Englishman. *Schoepf's Reise durch Pennsylvanien,* 1783, p. 185.

If there was a spring on his farm, which supplied him with water, he built a milk house, and, on the floor above, was a place to smoke meat, if not, a loft to store winter apples.—I. D. Rupp.

[33] After the first generation's houses of logs, which probably endured for twenty years, and the second and very substantial log structures, came the period of stone construction. These old stone homes, taverns and mansions, as they are found to-day yet on the streets of Germantown, and in such cities as Easton, Lancaster, and Lebanon, and as they stand in the midst of fertile farms, or by the road side as wayside inns, and the old, large, substantial and indestructible stone churches which still grace the landscape of the interior of eastern Pennsylvania, are worthy monuments, able to endure through all time, of the skill, the art, the industry and the resources of the early German inhabitants. The grandson of William Penn, passing through the region of the Tulpehocken, on April 10, 1788, wrote in his journal: "On the eastern side of this is a most elegant new Lutheran church. On the western is a Calvinist's, called here, by way of distinction, a Presbyterian church. After riding through a village (Hebron) I came to Lebanon, a handsome town, containing some hundred inhabitants. This place is decorated by a spire, and the houses are well built, many of them stone or brick."

[34] In dealing with William Penn, Pastorius and the Frankfort Land Company secured the choicest farming lands for the Ger-

ground. From an attention to the cultivation of grass, they often double the value of an old farm in a few years, and grow rich on farms, on which their predecessors[35] of whom they purchased them, have nearly starved. They prefer purchasing farms with some improvements[36] to settling a new tract of land.

---

mans. As, later, the migrations pressed westward of Chester County into the state, they took up the rich meadow lands of Montgomery, Lancaster, York, Lebanon, Berks, Lehigh, and portions of Bucks counties, leaving the hillsides to other nationalities. "The success of the German, in the first place, lay in this intuitive knowledge of good land. They almost invariably selected that which contained the heaviest timber, knowing that it would produce the largest crops, while many of the Scotch-Irish were no doubt intimidated by the herculean task of removing the heavy timber. . . . Another important factor in favor of the Germans was that which invariably led them to plow deep, and to keep the soil mellow at all times. They have always despised the 'yankee' methods of simply scratching the soil. . . . But no doubt the most important reason of this continued success lay in the fact that they never overtaxed the soil, but replenished it at regular intervals as carefully and generously as they fed their cattle."—Dr. George Mays, *The Early Pennsylvania-German Farmer, The Pennsylvania-German,* October, 1901, pp. 185, 186.

[35] The Germans have supplanted, in many counties, the Scotch-Irish. Cumberland, originally settled by Scotch-Irish, has now a prevailingly German population. In Northampton County, though there was at first a moiety of Irish or Scotch-Irish settlers; *now,* nine-tenths of the inhabitants are Germans. As early as 1790, Germans to the number of 145,000 were scattered through the State. Five-sixth of East Pennsylvania are Germans.—I. D. Rupp.

[36] Even in the small towns, "improvements" were a main fea-

3d. In clearing new land, they do not girdle[37] the trees simply, and leave them to perish in the ground, as is the custom of their English or Irish neighbors; but they generally cut them down and burn them. In destroying under-wood and bushes, they generally grub them out of the ground; by which means a field is as fit for cultivation the second year after it is cleared, as it is in twenty years afterwards. The advantages of this mode of clearing, consist in the immediate product of

---

ture. Gradually, back of the house there would be built a bake-oven, perhaps a wash-house, and a smoke-house, and on the rear of the lot a stable and pig sty. There would also be a large wood-pile and vegetable garden and sometimes a potato patch on each property.—Schmauk, *The Town of Steitz,* p. 48.

[37] The process of *girdling or belting,* was, to chop entirely around the tree, a curve of three or four inches wide. A tree was not well deadened unless it was cut to the red—cut completely through the *alburnum* or sap. Seventy years ago, when a piece of land was cleared in Cumberland County, in the first place, it was staked off by the *woodmen.* Provided with a *Wald-hacke,* grub-ax, he would take up by the roots die *Baeumchen,* the saplings, which he could shake in the root, by laying hold of the young tree, bending it backwards and forwards. If the roots yielded to this action, it was called a *grub.* After the land had been grubbed, the larger standing saplings, and trees were cut down, and chopped into rail lengths, of eleven feet or cordwood lengths, of four feet. The rail lengths were split for fencing purposes, the four feet lengths were split for firewood. This done, the brush was picked into heaps, and when dry, fire was set to them. The clearing, *das gelichtete Stueck,* was then ready for the plow.—I. D. Rupp.

the field, and in the greater facility with which it is ploughed, harrowed and reaped. The expense of repairing a plough, which is often broken two or three times in a year by small stumps concealed in the ground, is often greater than the extraordinary expense of grubbing the same field completely, in clearing it.[38]

4th. They feed their horses and cows, of which they keep only a small number, in such a manner, that the former perform twice the labor of those horses, and the latter yield twice the quantity of

---

[38] Those who practised *girdling or belting*, claimed that thus deadening the timber, had its advantages—labor was saved in chopping down and burning the stuff on the ground. In some parts of Pennsylvania, it was impossible to cut down the timber, because farmers were too poor to pay for so much labor. The dead timber afforded firewood for years, which obviated the necessity of resorting to the woods. When the deadened trees fell, the roots were taken out with the trees. In eight or ten years, the trees began to fall rapidly. When the ground was pretty well covered with old logs, the farmer commenced "to *nigger-off*," which was effected by laying the broken limbs and smaller trees across the logs and putting fire to it. The young members of the family, *boys and girls*, followed to *chunck up* the fires. In a few days, the logs were *niggered-off*, at the length of 12 or 15 feet. Sometimes the entire tree was consumed. When the logs were thus reduced to lengths that they could be handled by a few men, the owner had a *log-rolling*. He invited some of his neighbors, who assembled to aid him in his *rolling*. Usually, at such rollings, not a little hilarity prevailed, by reason of the free use of the German's *Brant-wein*, the Irishman's *uisge-beatha, usquebaugh*, the Frenchman's *Eau de vie*, water-of-life.—I. D. Rupp.

milk of those cows, that are less plentifully fed.[39] There is great economy in this practice, especially in a country where so much of the labour of a farmer is necessary to support his domestic animals. A German horse is known in every part of the state: indeed he seems to "feel with his lord, the pleasure and the pride" of his extraordinary size or fat.

5th. The fences of a German farm are generally high, and well built;[40] so that his fields seldom suffer from the inroads of his own or his neighbours, horses, cattle, hogs, or sheep.

6th. The German farmers are great economists of their wood. Hence they burn it only in stoves, in which they consume but a 4th or 5th part of what is commonly burnt in ordinary open fire places: besides, their horses are saved by means of this economy, from that immense labour, in hauling wood in the middle of winter, which frequently unfits the horses of their neighbours for the toils of the ensuing spring. Their houses are, moreover, rendered so comfortable, at all times, by large

---

[39] It is a maxim with Germans:

Mit Futtern ist Keine Zeit verloren,
i. e., To feed well, no time is lost.

Wer gut futtert — gut buttert,
i. e., He that feeds well, churns much butter.

—I. D. Rupp.

[40] Wie einer den Zaun haelt, haelt er auch das Gut,
i. e., The condition of the fence, shows the condition of the farm.

—I. D. Rupp.

close stoves,[41] that twice the business is done by every branch of the family, in knitting, spinning, and mending farming utensils, that is done in houses where every member of the family crowds near to a common fire-place, or shivers at a distance from it,—with hands and fingers that move, by reason of the cold, with only half their usual quickness.

They discover economy in the preservation and increase of their wood in several other ways. They sometimes defend it, by high fences, from their cattle; by which means the young forest trees are suffered to grow, to replace those that are cut down for the necessary use of the farm. But where this cannot be conveniently done, they surround the stump of that tree which is most useful for fences, viz., the chestnut, with a small triangular fence. From this stump a number of suckers shoot out in a few years, two or three of which in the course of five and twenty years, grow into trees of the

---

[41] In some of their houses, the Germans used the six-plate stove. Christopher Saur is said to have suggested the ten-plate stove. The cannon stoves first appeared in 1752 made at Lancaster and at Colebrookdale furnace, Berks County, and according to *Watson's Annals*, I., 218, they were used in churches and court rooms. Some of the earliest stoves in America, ten-plate, were made by Herr Huber, at "Elizabeth Hochofen," Lancaster County; of whom Baron Stiegel became the partner, after he came to this country from Mannheim, Germany, and to whom Huber sold his works in 1757. See *Der Deutsche Pioneer,* XVI., pp. 191–194; see also note 63a in this "Account."

same size as the tree from whose roots they derived their origin.

7th. They keep their horses and cattle as warm as possible in winter,[42] by which means they save a great deal of their hay and grain; for those animals when cold, eat much more than when they are in a more comfortable situation.

8th. The German farmers live frugally in their families, with respect to diet, furniture and apparel.[43] They sell their most profitable grain, which is wheat; and eat that which is less profitable, but more nourishing, that is, rye or Indian corn. The profit to a farmer, from this single article of economy, is equal, in the course of a life time, to the price of a farm for one of his children. They eat sparingly of boiled animal food, with large quantities of vegetable, particularly sallad, turnips, onions, and cabbage, the last of which

---

[42] The German Proverb runs:

Eine gute Kuh sucht man im Stalle,

i. e., One seeks for a good cow in the stable.

—I. D. Rupp.

[43] In an inventory of the goods of Andrew Ferree, a wealthy farmer of Lancaster County, appraised November 24, 1735, the following articles are enumerated, viz.: A large Family Bible, £2; two feather beds, £6; wearing clothes, £7; sundry pewter, £2, 8 shillings; a box of iron, 4 shillings; sundry ironware, £2; a watering pot, 6 shillings; wooden ware, £1; two iron pot racks, £1; two chests, 15 shillings; spinning wheel, 8 shillings; Total, £23, 1 shilling.—I. D. Rupp.

they make into sour crout.[44] They likewise use a large quantity of milk and cheese in their diet. Perhaps the Germans do not proportion the quantity of their animal food, to the degrees of their labour; hence it has been thought, by some people, that they decline in strength sooner than their English or Irish neighbors. Very few of them ever use distilled spirits in their families: their common drinks are cyder,[45] beer, wine, and simple water. The furniture of their house is plain and useful. They cover themselves in winter with light feather beds[46] instead of blankets; in this con-

[44] Sauer-kraut is a wholesome food, if properly made, and not allowed to ferment beyond the proper point. It had been, as some maintain, among the favorite dishes upon the table of Charlemagne (Karl der Grosse), king of France, who died A.D. 814, and very likely was made by the Germans, of the days of *Attila,* king of the Huns, who died A.D. 453. Throughout Germany it is served three or four times a week, during the winter.—I. D. Rupp.

[45] See "*The Old Cider Mill*" by Dr. S. P. Heilman, in *Proceedings of Lebanon County Historical Society,* Vol. II.

[46] Elkanah Watson, a New Englander, in a tour from Providence, R. I., to South Carolina, through Pennsylvania, in October, 1777, says: "At Reamstown (Lancaster Co., Pa.) I was placed between two beds, without sheets or pillows. This, as I was told, was a prevailing custom, but, which, as far as my experience goes, tends little to promote either the sleep or comfort of a stranger."—Elkanah Watson, *Men and Times,* p. 31.

A tourist writes from Toeplitz, a town and watering place in Bohemia, 1831: "At Berggrieshuebel, where we stopped for the night, we were introduced for the first time, to the stewing of a real *German bed.* It consists of two large bags filled with

trivance there is both convenience, and economy, for the beds are warmer than blankets, and they are made by themselves. The apparel of the German farmers is usually home spun.[47] When they use European articles of dress, they prefer those which are of the best quality, and of the highest price. They are afraid of debt, and seldom purchase anything without paying cash for it.[47a]

---

downs, between which, without any other covering, the luckless wight of a traveller is called to repose. How this *buttering on both sides* may do in the winter, I shall not determine; but, heaven knows, that on the occasion referred to, it was altogether insupportable. I endeavored, but failed, to get a couch more in unison with the atmosphere of summer; of course, I was obliged from sheer fatigue, to submit to the dissolution and thaw of this fearful hot bath."—Strang, *Germany,* p. 235.—Quoted by I. D. Rupp.

[47] The German farmer's motto is:

Selbstgesponnen, selbst-gemacht:
Rein dabei is Bauerntracht.

Poetized—

To spin, to weave, to ready make his clothes,
And keep them clean, the frugal farmer knows.

Carpets, now deemed indispensable to comfort, were not to be seen in a German farmer's house before 1800. There are still some Germans, especially among the Amish and German Brethren, who dispense with this comfort. Carpets were nowhere to be seen, in rooms or parlors, even in Philadelphia, till about 1750.—I. D. Rupp.

[47a] Dr. Rush furnishes a striking illustration of this fact in the following anecdote of Christopher Ludwick:

"At the close of the war, he returned and settled on his farm near Germantown. His house had been plundered of every article

9th. The German farmers have larger or profitable gardens near their houses. These contain little else but useful vegetables. Pennsylvania is indebted to the Germans for the principal part of her knowledge in horticulture. There was a time when turnips and cabbage were the principal vegetables that were used in diet by the citizens of Philadelphia. This will not surprise those persons, who know that the first English settlers in Pennsylvania left England while horticulture was in its

---

of furniture, plate and wearing apparel, he had left in it, by the British army on their march to Philadelphia. As he had no more cash than was sufficient to satisfy the demands of the market, he suffered a good deal from the want of many of the conveniences of life. He slept six weeks between blankets, rather than contract a single debt by replacing his sheets."—Rush, *Life of Ludwick.*

Ludwick received a commission signed by order of Congress by John Hancock President, as Superintendent of Bakers in the army of the United States. "When this commission was delivered to him by a committee of Congress, they proposed, that for every pound of flour, he should furnish the army with a pound of bread. 'No gentlemen,' said he, 'I will not accept of your commission upon any such terms; Christopher Ludwick does not want to get rich by the war; he has money enough. I will furnish one hundred and thirty-five pounds of bread for every cwt. of flour you put into my hands.' The committee were strangers to the increase of weight which flour acquires by the addition of water and leaven.

"From this time there were no complaints of the bad quality of bread in the army, nor was there a moment in which the movements of the army, or of any part of it, were delayed from the want of that necessary article of food."

General Washington addressed Ludwick as "his honest friend." —Rush, *Life of Ludwick,* pp. 14, 15.

infancy in that country. It was not until the reign of William III. that this useful and agreeable art was cultivated by the English nation. Since the settlement of a number of German gardeners in the neighborhood of Philadelphia, the tables of all classes of citizens have been covered with a variety of vegetables, in every season of the year; and to the use of these vegetables, in diet, may be ascribed the general exemption of the citizens of Philadelphia from diseases of the skin.

10th. The Germans seldom hire men to work upon their farms. The feebleness of that authority which masters possess over hired servants,[48] is such that their wages are seldom procured from their labour, except in harvest, when they work in the presence of their masters. The wives and daughters of the German farmers frequently forsake, for a while, their dairy and spinning-wheel, and join their husbands and brothers in the labour of cutting down, collecting and bringing home the fruits of their fields and orchards. The work of the gardens is generally done by the women of the family.[49]

---

[48] Unlike their English and Irish neighbors, they never, as a general thing, had colored servants, or slaves. Berks, a German County, having a population of 30,179, in 1790, had only 65 slaves in the ratio of one to 464 whites. Cumberland County, originally settled by Scotch-Irish, with a population in 1790 of 15,655, had 360 slaves, in the ratio of one to 44 whites.—I. D. Rupp.

[49] Times and customs have changed since the pristine settlements of Pennsylvania. Not more than seventy years ago, the good housewife aided by her daughters, would cultivate the gar-

11th. A large and strong waggon[50] covered with linen cloth, is an essential part of the furniture of a German farm. In this waggon, drawn by four or five large horses of a peculiar breed;[51] they con-

den, dress and keep it in order, decorate the cottage with choice honeysuckles, direct the tendrils of the native grapes that shaded the house. In the winter, mothers and daughters spun flax; in the spring, the wool, on the humming wheel; from the warp and weft of the spun yarn, they wove linen, linsey and woolen webs. Then a loom was found in every family. The linen, she spread in the proper season, upon the lawn, to whiten or bleach. Exposed alike with husband, the wife cheerfully bore with him the burden and toil of life. Even sixty years ago, there could be seen the *Baurbursch,* the youthful peasant, at the side of him, the *Baurmaedchen,* the peasant girl, the classic *Puella rustica,* wielding the sickle. Then, this season, *tempus messis,* harvest time, was one replete with more than ordinary interest to the youthful blood of both sexes, "redolent of joy and youth." In many parts of Germany, even at this day, the farmers' wives perform field labor, as well as the men.—I. D. Rupp.

[50] Schoepf, in speaking of the Market in Philadelphia, 1782, says: "Die entfernsten, besonders deutschen Landleute, kommen mit grossen, mit mancherlei Proviant beladenen bedeckten Waegen auf denen sie zugleich ihren eigenen Mundvorrath und Futter fuer ihre Pferde mit bringen, und darauf uebernachten," (p. 165); the most distant, especially German country people come to the city, with large covered wagons, laden with all sorts of provisions; bringing with them, at the same time, their own victuals, and feed for their horses, while remaining here.—I. D. Rupp.

[51] The peculiar breed was the Conestoga horse, of wide celebrity. The name Conestoga is from the name of a stream in Lancaster County, along which Swiss Mennonites settled, as early as 1709, 1717. They were principally farmers. When the Mennonites first settled in Conestoga valley, the counties of Phila-

vey to market over the roughest roads, between 2 or 3 thousand pounds weight of the produce of their farms. In the months of September and October, it is no uncommon thing, on the Lancaster and Reading roads, to meet in one day from fifty to an hundred of these waggons, on their way to Philadelphia, most of which belong to German farmers.[52]

12th. The favourable influence of agriculture, as conducted by the Germans in extending human happiness, is manifested by the joy they express upon the birth of a child. No dread of poverty, nor distrust of Providence from an increasing family, depress the spirits of these industrious and frugal people. Upon the birth of a son, they exult in the gift of a ploughman or a waggoner; and upon the birth of a daughter, they rejoice in the addition of another spinster, or milkmaid to their family. Happy state of human society! What

delphia and Chester had been settled by English emigrants, who brought some horses with them. From this stock, the Conestoga horse was derived.—*His. Lan. Co. Pa.*, pp. 74, etc.; *Rep. Com. of Agri.*, 1863, pp. 175, 180.—I. D. Rupp.

[52] In 1789, there were no turnpike roads in Pennsylvania. June 21, 1792, the Philadelphia and Lancaster Turnpike Co. was chartered, which made and established the first turnpike road laid in Pennsylvania. It was commenced 1792, finished 1794. It was sixty-two miles in length, and cost $7,500 per mile. The Germantown and Perkiomen turnpike road was begun 1801, finished 1804, 25 miles in length, cost $11,287 per mile.—I. D. Rupp. For early roads, see Ferree, *Pennsylvania*, pp. 209, 210.

blessings can civilization confer, that can atone for the extinction of the ancient and patriarchal pleasure of raising up a numerous and healthy family of children, to labour for their parents, for themselves, and for their country; and finally to partake of the knowledge and happiness which are annexed to existence! The joy of parents upon the birth of a child is the grateful echo of creating goodness. May the mountains of Pennsylvania be forever vocal, with songs of joy upon these occasions! They will be the infallible signs of innocence, industry, wealth and happiness of the state.[53]

13th. The Germans take great pains to produce, in their children, not only habits of labour, but a love of it. In this they submit to the irreversible sentence inflicted upon man, in such a manner, as to convert the wrath of heaven into public and private happiness. "To fear God, and to love work," are the first lessons they teach their children.[54] They prefer industrious habits to money

[53] Here is a prophecy, made in 1789 for Pennsylvania, and sufficiently vital to-day to form the text of an earnest sermon to the children who are departing from the ways of their fathers.

[54] The Germans believed:

> Muesiggang, ist des Teufels Ruhebank:
> An idle brain is the devil's workshop.

To their children, they said:

> Arbeite treu, und glaub es fest
> Dass Faulheit aerger ist als Pest,
> Der Muesiggang viel Boeses lehrt,
> Und alle Art von Suenden mehrt.

itself; hence, when a young man asks the consent of his father to marry the girl of his choice, he does not enquire so much whether she be rich or poor, or whether she possesses any personal or mental accomplishments—as whether she be industrious, and acquainted with the duties of a good house-wife?[55]

14th. The Germans set a great value upon patrimonial property. This useful principle in human nature prevents much folly and vice in young people. It moreover leads to lasting and extensive

---

Work faithfully: believe 'tis true,
Idleness is worse than a pest;
It is sure, much harm to do,
The cause of gross sins, 'tis confest.

—I. D. Rupp.

The eighty-eighth of Christopher Dock's *One Hundred Necessary Rules for Conduct of Children* ran, "Be never idle, but either go to assist your parents, or recite your lessons, and learn by heart what was given you."—Schantz, *Proceedings of the Pennsylvania-German Society,* X., 96.

[55] German maxims:

Ein fleissige Hausfrau ist die beste Sparbuechse.
An industrious house-wife is the best money-safe.

Erwerben, un sparen zugleich
Macht am gewissesten reich.

He that earns and *Saves* will be,
Rich for certain, you shall see.

Der Ehestand ist ein Huehner haus
Der eine will hinein, der andre will heraus.

The marriage state is like a coop, built stout,
The *outs* would fain be in, the *ins* be out.

—I. D. Rupp.

advantages, in the improvement of a farm; for what inducement can be stronger in a parent to plant an orchard,[56] to preserve forest trees or to build a commodious and durable house, than the idea, that they will all be possessed by a succession of generations, who shall inherit his blood and name.

15th. The German farmers are very much influenced in planting and pruning trees, also in sowing and reaping, by the age and appearances of the moon. This attention to the state of the moon has been ascribed to superstition;[57] but if the facts re-

---

[56] The German axiom reads:

> Im kleinsten Raum pflanz einen Baum
> Und pflege sein, er bringt dir's ein.
>
> In smallest space, a fruit tree place,
> Attend it well, have fruit to sell.
>
> —I. D. Rupp.

[57] The dependence of the Pennsylvania-German farmer upon the almanac for major and minor agricultural operations, as well as for many activities of the household, and the faith in proverbs and superstitions connected with the signs of the zodiac, and particularly with the phases of the moon, is well known, and continues in some measure to the present time. In how far climatic influences are to be ascribed to the influence of celestial bodies, in addition to that of the sun, and how far the superstitious folk-lore of the Pennsylvania-Germans is dependent upon the tissue of superstition which was universal in the Old World from which they came, has not yet been accurately determined. But, doubtless, much of their implicit faith even in superstitions is due to the respect which they had for the forces of Providence and Nature, as able to control, to guide, and to destroy the most

lated by Mr. Wilson in his observations upon climates are true, part of their success in agriculture must be ascribed to their being so much influenced by it.

16th. From the history that has been given of the German agriculture, it will hardly be necessary to add that a German farm may be distinguished from the farms of the other citizens of the state, by the superior size of their barns;[58] the plain, but compact form of their houses;[59] the height of their

---

powerful of the efforts of man. Long generations of experience generalized and summed up, often in fantastic manner, in folklore, was the sort of wisdom on which these keen and hardy agricultural folk were obliged to depend, in lieu of anything better, for their agricultural operations.

[58] See Note 30.

[59] The inferiority of the house, and the home, and its appointments, to those of the farm and the barn, is a criticism most frequently urged against the Pennsylvania-Germans, and is found amplified into larger principles of life, in such works as *Tillie, the Mennonite Maid.* In an impartial investigation into this limitation of the Pennsylvania-German character, it should, however, be remembered that their life in the open air, their healthy robustness in toil, their joy in labor and in its success, and the necessity of looking to the substantial returns of the soil overshadowed the life within the house, which was really and chiefly a resting place and a shelter against the extremities of the weather. The real life of the Pennsylvania-German was in work out of doors, and his real home was not his house, but his farm. This outlook of his is narrow and defective, it is true, but not more so —and perhaps less—than the modern outlook becoming so prevalent now throughout America, in which the home is subordinated to the *street,* and the real life and enjoyment of youth

inclosures; the extent of their orchards; the fertility of their fields; the luxuriance of their meadows, and a general appearance of plenty and neatness in everything that belongs to them.

---

and of the people is not found in work in the heart of nature, but in enjoyment on excursions, sea-side allurements, automobile trips, shows, and theatricals.

THE MECHANICS AND MERCHANTS.

THE German mechanic possesses some of the traits of the character that has been drawn of the German farmer. His first object is to become a freeholder;[60] and hence we find few of them live in rented houses.[61] The highest compliment that can be paid to them on entering their houses is to ask them, "is this house your own." They are industrious, frugal,[62] punctual

[60] It is the German element in many American cities and towns that gives the community a large share of the aggregate wealth, reliability and independence.

[61] The reverse of this quality is found in that American citizen to-day who is willing to mortgage his ancestral home in order to purchase a motor car.

[62] The impression that the Germans made upon the keen eye of Benjamin Rush was not one of avarice or meanness, and in drawing a moral in his *Life of Christopher Ludwick* he says (pp. 5, 6): "The history of the life and character of Christopher Lud-

and just. Since their settlement in Pennsylvania, many of them have acquired a knowledge of those mechanical arts, which are more immediately necessary and useful in a new country; while they continue at the same time, to carry on the arts[63] they imported from Germany, with vigour and success.[63a]

---

wick, is calculated to show the influence of a religious education upon moral conduct; of habits of industry and economy, upon success in all enterprises; and to inspire hope and exertion in young men of humble employment, and scanty capital, to aspire to wealth and independence, as the only means by which they are capable of commanding respect and affording happiness."

[63] Luetscher, *Industries of Pennsylvania after the Adoption of the Federal Constitution, with special reference to Lancaster and York Counties, Americana Germanica,* vol. v, pp. 135–155, and pp. 197–208. See also the *Danner Museum* at Mannheim.

The German aptitude for thoroughness, for patience, for system and order, for a willingness to wait until the proper time has arrived in which to carry on any particular stage of an enterprise, and the absence of that nervous haste and feverish zeal to see immediate results, which characterizes more mercurial races, has always been charged to the account of the Pennsylvania-German's slowness. It is quite true that he cannot and will not be hurried; but it is equally true that his work in the mechanical arts, when once done, need not be done over again. The results are worth the additional time spent in the process. This is one of the secrets of the Pennsylvania-German's success in dealing with Nature, who will not allow herself to be hurried, and does not approve of man's impatience, in the growth of crops.

[63a] Both the paper making and the printing industry in Pennsylvania were founded by Germans. Throughout the rural districts they set up grist mills and saw mills. Many of them were weavers. The Pennsylvania Gazette of March 5, 1730, tells us that the German Mennonite Kurtz built his iron works on *Octorara*

But the genius of the Germans of Pennsylvania, is not confined to agriculture and the mechanical arts. Many of them have acquired great wealth by foreign and domestic commerce. As merchants[64] they are candid and punctual. The bank

---

Creek, in Lancaster County, as early as 1726. The "*Oley*" works were founded in 1745. The Tulpehocken "*Eisenhammer,*" two miles from Womelsdorf, was established in 1749. The iron smelting industry at *Elizabeth,* on the southern slope of the Cornwall hills, with Schaefferstown on the one side, and Mannheim on the other, was founded by Herr Johann Huber in 1750, who in 1757 sold his works to Baron H. W. Stiegel. This plant included not only a smelting furnace, but a foundry, smith shops, a wagon factory, and more extensive than all, an establishment for the manufacture of iron plates for stoves, which are said to have borne the inscription:

"Baron Stiegel ist der Mann
Der die Oefen giessen kann."

Wollenweber claims (*Der Deutsche Pionier,* II., p. 28) he saw a stove in Lebanon with this inscription shortly before 1870. For Baron Stiegel, see *Der Deutsche Pionier,* XII., pp. 82–87; also *A Tale,* by M. H. Stine, Ph.D., Philadelphia, 1903.

[64] The sense of honor, of responsibility to the public, and of carrying on a business, whether by large or small expenditure, in the way that is proper to that particular piece of business, has always been remarkable among this people. Dr. Rush detected it in the public business activities of Christopher Ludwick. He says (pp. 18, 19): "I have known Christopher Ludwick from an early period in the war, and have every reason to believe, as well from observation as information, that he has been a true and faithful servant to the public; that he has detected and exposed many impositions, which were attempted to be practised by others in his department; that he has been the cause of much saving in many respects; and that his deportment in public life, has afforded unquestionable proofs of his integrity and worth.

of North America has witnessed, from its first institution, their fidelity to all their pecuniary engagements.[65]

"With respect to his losses, I have no personal knowledge, but have often heard that he has suffered from his zeal in the cause of his country."

[65] The word "German" or "German-American" to-day, in connection with a bank, a real estate agency, a building association, or any semi-public financial enterprise, still carries with it some feeling that there is good management, prudence, skill in investment, safety of capital, and returns in interest, to be expected. The German character, when uncorrupted, regards the discharge of a financial obligation or responsibility, as a point of duty and of honor, as of first importance, and to be toiled for patiently, until the end has been realized.

GENERAL CHARACTERISTICS.

THUS far I have described the individual character of several orders of the German citizens of Pennsylvania. I shall now take notice of some of their manners[66] in a collective capacity. All the different sects among them are particularly attentive to the religious education[67] of their children, and to the establishment and support of the Christian Religion. For this purpose they settle as much as

[66] See remarks on the use of this word in the Introduction to this "Account."

[67] THE SCHOOLS OF THE PENNSYLVANIA GERMANS.

There was almost no illiteracy among the original immigrants, and during the whole period of immigration, Germans educated in German universities were coming to this country. Pastorius, Köster, Weis, Peter Miller, Muhlenberg, Schlatter and Kunze were all active in the Province of Pennsylvania (compare

Kurz gefaßte.

Nützliches

Schul=Büchlein

Die kinder zu unterrichten, in Buchstabieren, Lesen, und auswendig lernen,

---

Deme angehänget ein kurzer doch deutlicher, und gründlicher

Unterricht
Zur Rechenkunst.

Aufgesetzt zum Nutz und Gebräuch vor Kinder.

Von L. H

Zweyte Auflage.

EPHRATA.

Gedruckt und zu bekommen bey dem Schulmeister, Drucker und Buchbinder 1786

LUDWIG HOECKER'S PENNSYLVANIA-GERMAN SCHOOL TEXTBOOK giving instruction in spelling, reading and arithmetic, together with passages for memorizing, and printed at the Ephrata Press in 1786, three years before Dr. Rush wrote his work on the Germans.

possible together—and make the erection of a school house and a place of worship the first object

Rosengarten, *Proceedings of Pennsylvania-German Society,* XIII., 65); but, as Muhlenberg observes, the original immigrants were so absorbed with the preparation of the soil and the erection of buildings, that the second and the third generation did not receive the same training that had been given to their parents, and were growing up wild and untutored. Yet the pastors and the school masters did their best under prevailing conditions, and sent pleas to Europe for help.

Christopher Dock opened a school on the Skippack for the Mennonites as early as 1718 and wrote his Schul-Ordnung in 1750. Ludwick Hecker taught the children of the Dunkards at Ephrata in 1739. In 1743 the Moravians under the direction of Count Zinzendorf opened day schools at such places as Muddy Creek, Lancaster, Oley, Mill Creek, Warwick, Heidelberg, Macungie, and Germantown, and also conducted boarding schools. In 1748 the Lutherans had a school and teacher in Philadelphia, in Germantown two schools and teachers, in Providence a small school, in New Holland a rather large school and a teacher, in Lancaster two school teachers and seventy children. In 1749, no less than twelve school masters arrived, and in 1750 came Gottlieb Mittelberger. The ministers and the younger candidates for the ministry organized and taught schools among the people. The *Hallesche Nachrichten* frequently refer to the work and the difficulties of the school masters among whom J. Nicholas Kurtz and Jacob Loeser may especially be mentioned. In 1758 the Swedish Lutheran pastor Acrelius wrote: "In almost every ridge is a school house. . . . None, whether boys or girls, are now growing up who cannot read English, write and cipher." This certainly is too roseate a view of the situation.

Shortly after the middle of the century, the Charity School Movement, which was an effort to educate the Germans in Pennsylvania in the English language by endowment funds from Eng-

of their care. They commit the education and instruction of their children in a peculiar manner to the ministers and officers of their churches;—hence

---

land, with the ultimate view, by some of those connected with the movement, of bringing the children into the Anglican Church, arose, and, with its offer of hope, perhaps somewhat unfortunately, dominated the situation for a time. Before the end of the century, however, the Germans had returned to the parochial plan, and very large parochial schools, supported by popular subscription in the congregation, were created for the education of the youth in such cities and towns as Philadelphia, Lancaster, Reading and Lebanon. In 1793, four years after Dr. Rush wrote his "Account," the Lutheran Ministerium of Pennsylvania reports forty-six schools in twenty-one parishes, of which ten were in Philadelphia. The minutes of the conventions show that a report of the condition of the schools was required of the ministers annually at the meeting of the body. Barr Ferree in his excellent *Pennsylvania: A Primer,* New York, 1904, pp. 230, 231, does justice to the Friends, the Episcopalians, the Presbyterians, and the Moravians, but not to the Reformed Lutheran and Germans, where he also mistakenly identifies the idea of the "Union Church" with the early schools. Earlier in his work (p. 101), speaking of the Germans, he says: "As a whole they were not opposed to education, and established schools from the earliest date. Michael Schlatter and Henry Melchior Muhlenberg, the leaders of the Reformed and Lutheran Germans, were in favor of the higher education."

Any effort to deal with "the Germans as an increasingly illiterate or irreligious people necessarily met their disapproval. They were too conscientious, too frank, too self-respecting, to tolerate any attempt at assistance, when assistance was the expression, on the part of their would-be benefactors, of a mistaken interpretation of their character, and on their own part a confession of weaknesses that did not exist. Dr. William Smith and his English allies did not understand these Pennsylvania-German immigrants. . . .

they grow up with prejudices in favour of public worship, and of the obligations of Christianity. Such has been the influence of a pious education[68] among the German Lutherans[69] in Pennsylvania, that in the course of nineteen years,[70] only one of them has ever been brought to a place of public shame or punishment.[71]

As members of civil government, the Germans

"The Germans were not opposed to schools. That was not the issue. They loved their own national inheritances, their religious freedom, their educational ideals, including their mother-tongue. For these they resolutely struggled and won. No educational struggle in Colonial America can at all compare with this."—M. G. Brumbaugh, in Weber, *The Charity School Movement.*

For the schools of the Germans in Pennsylvania, see *Hallesche Nachrichten,* I., 209, 234, 418, 431, 484, 551, 696; II., 38, 178, 218, 480, 559, 627, 629, 637, 661, 1476, 1477; *Coetus of the Reformed Congregations,* Charity Schools, 129, passim to 220; High School at Lancaster, 392, 403, 404, 409, 411, 426, 441; Brumbaugh, *Life and Works of Christopher Dock,* Philadelphia, Lippincott Company, 1908; Weber, *The Charity School Movement in Colonial Pennsylvania,* 1754–1763, Philadelphia, W. J. Campbell, 1905.

[68] This education was very much more thorough than that of our own day, in rooting the impulses of conduct deeply in the fear and love of God.

[69] The text of I. D. Rupp omits the word "Lutherans."

[70] This is the generation trained by Muhlenberg, Brunnholtz, Handschuh, and the pious and indefatigable line of ministers from Halle.

[71] Dr. Rush was intimate with the German pastors and the German people in Philadelphia among whom he moved as a physician, and must have known whereof he spoke.

are peaceable[72]—and exact in the payment of their taxes.[73] Since they have participated in the power of the state,[74] many of them have become sensible

[72] There is an element of respect for authority, of willingness to share and bear the common burden, and of silence rather than remonstrance under the petty injustices and frictions in the common affairs of civil life, as well as a sense of loyalty, and a feeling of gratitude, which render the unsophisticated country-German character an exceedingly desirable and valuable element in the citizenship of any state.

If a citizen of a state be valuable to it on account of "his faithful obedience to the laws or for the sacredness with which he preserves the family compact, our German farmers certainly merit as much as any other class for the practice of these virtues." —*Philadelphia Ledger*, 1856, quoted by I. D. Rupp.

[73] It has been well said: "One of our richest men invariably spreads his *papers* before the assessor, and tells him to tax him, according to his mind. A genuine Pennsylvania-German buys for cash; or never, unless he sees the avenue by which the means are to flow into his hands. Our wives do not own their husband's property. Pedlers and venders lose less among us, than by other folks." *C. Z. W. Ref. Church Messenger*, 1868.—I. D. Rupp.

[74] See address of George F. Baer, *Proceedings of Pennsylvania-German Society*, I., pp. 18–25; Egle, *Place of the Pennsylvania-German in the Commonwealth, Proceedings of the Pennsylvania-German Society*, II., 18–130; Richards, *Pennsylvania-Germans in the French and Indian War, Proceedings of the Pennsylvania-German Society*, V.; Rosengarten, *Soldiers in the Revolution, Proceedings of the Pennsylvania-German Society*, XIII.; Heckman, *Soldiers in the Revolution, Proceedings of the Pennsylvania-German Society*, XI., pp. 8–12; Richards, *The Pennsylvania-Germans in the Revolutionary War, Proceedings of the Pennsylvania-German Society*, VII.; Address by S. W.

and enlightened in the science of legislation. Pennsylvania has had the speaker's chair of her assembly,[75] and the vice-president's office of her council,[76] filled with dignity by gentlemen of German families. The same gentlemen have since been advanced to seats in the house of representatives,[77]

Pennypacker, *Proceedings of the Pennsylvania-German Society,* IX.; Address by John Wanamaker, *Proceedings of the Pennsylvania-German Society,* XIX.

When Rev. Peter Muhlenberg received a commission from General Washington, he preached a farewell sermon to his congregation, depicting the wrongs this country had suffered from Great Britain, and then exclaimed, "There is a time for all things—a time to preach and a time to pray; but there is also a time to fight and that time has now come." After pronouncing the benediction he threw off his gown, and was in full military uniform. Proceeding to the door of the church, he ordered the drums to beat for recruits and nearly three hundred of his congregation responded to the appeal. He at once marched to the relief of Charleston, and was engaged at the Brandywine, Germantown, Monmouth, Stony Point and Yorktown. Though he and his congregation were situated in Woodstock, Virginia, they were Pennsylvania-Germans.

[75] Frederick Augustus Conrad Muhlenberg, twice Speaker of the Pennsylvania Legislature.

[76] General Peter Muhlenberg, Vice-President of the Council during the Presidency of Benjamin Franklin, who was enfeebled by age.

[77] Frederick Augustus Conrad Muhlenberg was twice Speaker of the United States House of Representatives. He also had been a member of the Continental Congress. General Peter Muhlenberg was a member of the First, Second, and Third Congress, serving from 1789 to 1795. He was elected again, and served from 1799 to 1801. In the same year he was chosen to the United States Senate but resigned.

under the new constitution of the United States. In the great controversy about the national government, a large majority of the Germans in Pennsylvania decided in favour of its adoption,[78] notwithstanding the most popular arts were used to prejudice them against it.

The Germans are but little addicted to convivial pleasures.

They seldom meet for the simple purpose of eating and drinking in what are justly called "feeding parties"; but they are not strangers to the virtue of hospitality. The hungry or benighted traveller,

[78] This was the controversy through which Pennsylvania had just passed when Dr. Rush wrote his *Account,* a controversy in which he was deeply interested.

Dr. Rush does not directly allude to the Revolutionary War in this *Account.* We have summed up the services of the Pennsylvania-Germans in the War of Independence in *Note* 127. Though silent as to the great conflict through which his country had passed and in which he had been a participant, Dr. Rush in his *Life of Christopher Ludwick* describes Ludwick's patriotism as follows:

"He possessed at that time, nine houses in Philadelphia, a farm near Germantown, and three thousand five hundred pounds, Pennsylvania currency, at interest; all of which he staked with his life, in the scale of his country. He was elected successively a member of all the Committees and Conventions, which conducted the affairs of the Revolution, in Pennsylvania, in 1774, 1775, and 1776. His principles and conduct were alike firm, under the most difficult and alarming events of those memorable years."

"A general conviction of the ardor and sincerity of his patriotism procured him at once the offer of a chair or a seat at the dinner table wherever he went."—Rush, *Life of Ludwick.*

is always sure to find a hearty welcome under their roofs.[79] A gentleman of Irish extraction, who lost his way in travelling through Lancaster county, called late at night at the door of a German farmer. He was kindly received and entertained with the best of everything the house afforded. The next morning, he offered to pay his host for his lodging, and other accommodation: " No " said the friendly German, in broken English—" I will take nothing from you. I was once lost, and entertained, as you have been, at the house of a stranger who would take no pay from me for his trouble. I am therefore now only discharging that debt:—do you pay your debt to me in the same way to somebody else."[80]

They are extremely kind and friendly as neighbours. They often assist each other by loans of money for a short time, without interest, when the purchase of a plantation makes a larger sum necessary than is commonly possessed by a single farmer. To secure their confidence, it is necessary to be

---

[79] Tacitus, in his *De Moribus Germaniæ,* says: " The master of the house welcomes every stranger, and regales him to the best of his ability. When his provisions are exhausted, he goes to his neighbor, conducts his new acquaintance to another hospitable board. They do not wait to be invited; are received most cordially. Between an intimate friend and a stranger no distinction is made."—I. D. Rupp.

[80] The most liberal hospitality and disinterestedness mark the character of the Germans in Europe. *Goldsmith's Manners and Customs of Nations,* p. 64—I. D. Rupp.

punctual.[81] They never lend money a second time, to a man who has once disappointed them in paying what he had borrowed agreeably to his promise or obligation. It was remarked, during the late war, that there were very few instances of them discharging a bond, or a debt, with depreciated paper money.

It has been said, that the Germáns are deficient in learning;[82] and that in consequence of their want

---

81 Wer puenctlich bezahlt, mag wieder borgen.
He that pays punctually can borrow again.
Koerte's Sprichwoerter.—I. D. Rupp.

I recall an old Pennsylvania-German, a professional man of high culture and character, who agreed to loan a sum of money to an acquaintance who said he would call for it on a certain day at 1 P. M. The man appeared a few minutes after 1 and was told that he could not have the loan, since a man who was ten minutes late in an appointment in which he was to receive money, would be sure to be late when the time came to paying it back.

82 It must never be forgotten that the whole legal, technical and political frame of activities in Pennsylvania was being conducted in a language with which the Germans were imperfectly familiar, and that, therefore, though many of them were intelligent, thoughtful, and well educated, they were unable to express themselves on points at issue to those round about them. They were right, far more so than the Quakers and the Tories, on all the large issues of the day, and they relied upon their leaders for information and for advice.

Says Barr Ferree (*Pennsylvania Primer*): "Schlatter was the leader of the Reformed. . . . Muhlenberg became the leader of the Lutherans in Pennsylvania and in the colonies. These two men with Saur of Germantown with his newspaper were the three leaders of opinion among the Germans in colonial Pennsylvania."

of more general and extensive education, they are much addicted to superstition,[83] and are frequently imposed upon in the management of their affairs.

Many of them have lost valuable estates by being unacquainted with the common forms of law,[84] in

---

It was John Peter Miller of little inland Ephrata who translated the Declaration of Independence into seven languages for the Continental Congress.

For certain reasons the Pennsylvania-Germans have suffered more than other stocks under the charge of ignorance preferred by the native American element, which does not understand them. It is so to this day. For the influence exerted by German thought on *American Education,* see Faust, *The German Element In The United States,* 1909, Vol. II., Chap. V.

[83] They were not at all superstitious in the sense of harboring fear, and they became suspicious of those who thought them over-credulous; but their largeness and even excess of faith in the supernatural, and the confidence and trust they reposed in men whom they looked to as leaders, caused them very frequently to be taken advantage of by men to whom they entrusted their affairs.

The history and traditions of their forefathers would tend to make the Pennsylvania-German feel that he would probably be taken advantage of, in business, at the hand of the stranger.

At the very start of their career as emigrants, many of them had been deceived by the flashy *Neulander,* and by the unworthy leaders given them by the *Neulander.* They had been obliged to work in the tar camps in New York, they had been sold as Redemptioners in Pennsylvania.

[84] Such losses are met with to-day yet on the part of very intelligent and highly educated people, who, however, are devoid of business instinct and training, and who repose all their confidence in their business agents. To expect an acquaintance with

the most simple transactions; and many more of them have lost their lives, by applying to quacks[85] in sickness: but this objection to the Germans will soon cease to have any foundations in Pennsylvania. Several young men,[86] born of German parents, have been educated in law, physic,[87] and divinity,[88] who

---

the common forms of law on the part of the German immigrants is setting the goal very high.

[85] Dr. Rush was a physician. Although he himself, in many places in his writings, testifies to the primitive and unreliable character of the science of medicine in his day, yet here he shows a proper professional antipathy to those who set themselves up as skilled in the science of healing, without possessing the necessary qualifications or credentials. However, it is not only ignorant German immigrants in the eighteenth century, but very intelligent Americans of the twentieth century who resort to quack prescriptions and patent medicines in time of illness.

[86] Dr. Rush is doubtless referring to young Germans of the second generation who were at that time enrolled in the University of Pennsylvania. He penned these words in 1789, and a few years later, there graduated from the University of Pennsylvania one of these young men, George Lochman, who became a predecessor of the present writer in the Lutheran parish at Lebanon. Of the nine or ten pastors who have guided this old Pennsylvania-German parish during a century and a half, at least six have been graduates of universities.

[87] There lived at Hilspach, not far from Neckar Gemuend, near Heidelberg, Johannes Caspar Wuester—two of his sons emigrated to Pennsylvania; Caspar, in 1717, and Johannes, in 1727. Of the grandson of Caspar, Davenport says: " Caspar Wistar, a celebrated physician, was born in Philadelphia in 1761. He studied medicine under Dr. John Redman, and completed his professional course at the schools in London and Edinburgh. Returning in 1787 to his native city, he soon distinguished him-

have demonstrated by their abilities and knowledge, that the German genius for literature has not depreciated in America. A college has lately been founded by the state in Lancaster,[89] and committed chiefly to the care of the Germans of all sects, for

self in his profession, and in 1789 was elected professor of chemistry in the college of Philadelphia. In 1792 he became adjunct professor of anatomy, midwifery and surgery, with Dr. Shippen; and, on the decease of that gentleman, in 1808, sole professor. His acquirements in professional knowledge were very extensive, and he obtained much popularity as a lecturer. His chief work is a valuable system of *Anatomy, in two volumes.* He died 1819."—I. D. Rupp.

[88] Students of the Rev. Dr. John Christopher Kunze, a graduate of the University of Leipsig, who was professor of German and the Oriental Languages in 1780, and professor of Oriental Languages and Literature in Columbia College, New York, from 1784 on. He was the most influential advocate of the use of the English language by the Germans in this country in religious and other public gatherings, and issued the first English Lutheran Hymnal in America.

[89] The Assembly passed the act to incorporate Franklin and Marshall College on March 10, 1787, on the ground that "the citizens of this state of German birth or extraction, have eminently contributed by their industry, economy and public virtues to raise the state to its present happiness and prosperity." The act declares one of the purposes of the college to be "that the youth shall be taught in German, English, Latin, Greek and other learned languages." For further information as to the origin of this college see Dubbs, *History of the Reformed Church, Proceedings of the Pennsylvania German Society,* XI.; Schmauk, *History of the Lutheran Church in Pennsylvania, Proceedings of the Pennsylvania-German Society,* XI.; Dubbs, *History of Franklin and Marshall College* (1903).

the purpose of diffusing learning among their children. In this college[89a] they are to be taught the German and English languages, and all those branches of literature which are usually taught in the colleges of Europe and America. The principal of this college is a native of Pennsylvania, of German parentage. His extensive knowledge and taste in the arts and sciences, joined with his industry in the discharge of the duties of his station, have afforded to the friends of learning in Pennsylvania, the most flattering prospects of the future importance and usefulness of this institution.[90]

Both sexes of the Germans discover a strong propensity to vocal and instrumental music.[91] They

---

[89a] This college is named after Dr. Franklin, who was president of the State at the time it was founded, and who contributed very liberally to its funds.

[90] Henry Ernst Muhlenberg, pastor of Trinity Lutheran Church, Lancaster, the most learned botanist in America, and known as such throughout Europe, of the eighteenth century. His work on grasses, written in the Latin language, is still a high authority. With him was associated the Rev. Frederick Melsheimer, whose collection of insects was so complete that it was purchased by Harvard University as late as 1860.

To these learned Pennsylvania-Germans should be added such scientists as David Rittenhaus, who discovered the compensating pendulum, and the author on the Fungi of North America who discovered twelve hundred species new to science, who came from Nazareth; and William Audenried, who originated the plan of public education in our country.

[91] The Moravians of Bethlehem not only excelled in vocal and all orchestral music, but produced the greatest line of pipe organ

excel, in psalmody, all the other religious societies in the state.[92]

---

builders in America, culminating in David Tannenberger. The Germans of Pennsylvania were the best singers in the commonwealth. As early as 1750 Gottlieb Mittelberger brought an organ from Heilbronn, Germany, for the St. Michael's Lutheran Church in Philadelphia, and at the time when Dr. Rush was active, the largest organ in the United States, built by Tannenberger, stood in the German Zion Lutheran Church in Philadelphia.

[92] The singing in the German churches, often with organs, is noted by local chroniclers as remarkable, in certain of the old records that have come down to us from the past.

On this subject see also Sachse, *The Music of the Ephrata Cloister, Proceedings of the Pennsylvania-German Society,* XII., pp. 6–106.

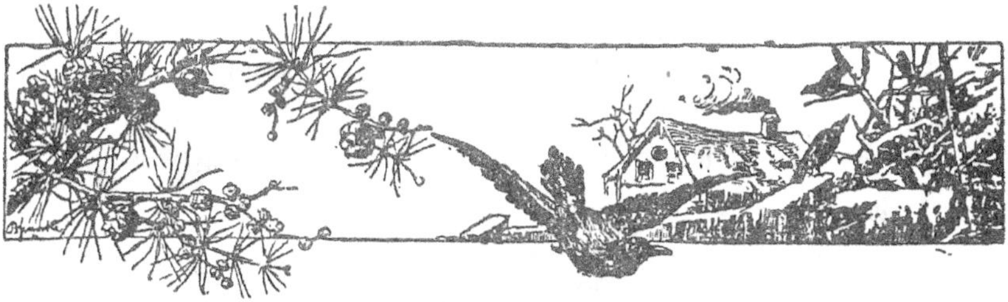

THE RELIGIOUS BODIES.[93]

THE freedom and toleration of the govern-

[93] "The Church encountered, at her entrance on this western world, the difficulty connected with the diversity of language. The song of Zion was to be sung in a strange land—where its sweetest utterances seemed a jargon and a babbling. They could not understand her testimony; they knew not of her rich literature, and of her glorious history; and when the poor German tried, in soul-deep utterances, to show that he had the same faith as Christ's people around him, they forgot the faith, and laughed at the broken utterances of his unhabituated lips. He knew his mother tongue too well to be laughed out of the heritage it brought him, and clung to it with a tenacity, religious, and sometimes almost fanatical. One national life was to pass over into another; the warm-hearted, simple-minded German was to be shaped in the mould of a harder national type. Our nation is not specially endowed with the faculty of entering into the peculiarities of others, and doing them justice. We have too determined a disposition to think well of ourselves. . . . Many of the German emigrants were poor, and in perpetual danger of becoming absorbed in purely material interests.

ment has produced a variety[93a] of sects, among the Germans in Pennsylvania.

The Lutherans compose a great proportion of the German citizens of the state.[94] Many of their churches are large and splendid.[95] The German

---

"Never was there such a harvest with so few laborers. It took a strong constitution to bear such an acclimation as she was called to pass through; but the Church still not only breathes, she *lives.*" —Charles Porterfield Krauth, in Spaeth, *Life of Krauth,* Vol. II., p. 42.

[93a] Penn's frame of government expressly provided this religious freedom. William Penn himself, speaking the German language well, was the personal originator of the German settlements in Pennsylvania. He visited the Fatherland three times in the interest of immigration and heartily welcomed the first immigrants to his forest province. It was he who was ultimately responsible for the transplanting of such a variety of religious belief.

[94] The statistics of the Ministerium of Pennsylvania show that in 1793 the two pastors in Philadelphia, whom Dr. Rush knew, viz., Dr. Helmuth and Rev. Schmidt, had 1996 communicants. The Lutheran Church has lost large numbers, because of its Germanic character, in the State of Pennsylvania, and the Reformed Church has given many members to the Presbyterian and other denominations. On the history of the Lutheran Church in Pennsylvania see the *Documentary History of the Ministerium of Pennsylvania; Hallesche Nachrichten,* by Mann and Schmucker, Allentown, Pa., 1886, two volumes; new edition, General Council Publication House, Philadelphia; Schmauk, *History of the Lutheran Church in Pennsylvania,* 1903, General Council Publication House, Philadelphia.

[95] "Let us," said Mr. Ludwick, "take them to Philadelphia, and there show them our fine German churches."—Rush, *Life of Christopher Ludwick,* p. 12.

Presbyterians are the next to them in numbers.[96] Their churches are likewise large and furnished, in many places, with organs. The clergy, belonging to these churches, have moderate salaries, but they are punctually and justly paid. In the country they have glebes which are stocked and occasionally worked by their congregations. The extra expenses of their ministers, in all their excursions to their ecclesiastical meetings, are borne by their respective congregations. By this means the discipline and

---

The Zion Lutheran Church, on Fourth and Cherry Street, Philadelphia, was the largest religious edifice in America. It was destroyed by fire after the Christmas festivities held in the church, five years after Dr. Rush's "*Account*" was written. On December 28, 1794, Dr. Rush placed the following note in his diary: "Met Dr. Helmuth going into St. Michael's Church on Fifth Street and condoled with him on the burning of his church on the evening of December 26. He said that it belonged to this world and he hoped that it would be the means of building up the invisible Church of Christ." The church was rebuilt, and in it were held the funeral services of George Washington in the presence of Congress, and Richard Henry Lee's resolutions were read, concluding with the declaration that the deceased had been "first in war, first in peace, and first in the hearts of his fellow-citizens."

[96] On the history of the Reformed Church see *Minutes and Letters of the Coetus of the German Reformed Congregations in Pennsylvania, 1747–1792, edited by Good and Hinke, Reformed Church Publication Board, Philadelphia, 1903;* Dubbs, *History of the Reformed Church,* 1895; Dubbs, *The Reformed Church in Pennsylvania, in Proceedings of Pennsylvania-German Society,* Vol. XI.; Dotterer, *Historical Notes Relating to the Pennsylvania Reformed Church,* Philadelphia, 1900. See also the *Researches* of Professor Hinke.

general interests of their churches are preserved and promoted. The German Lutherans and Presbyterians live in great harmony with each other, insomuch that they often preach in each other's churches and in some instances unite in building a church, in which they both worship at different times.[97] This harmony between two sects, one so much opposed to each other, is owing to the relaxation of the Presbyterians in some of the peculiar doctrines of Calvinism.[98] I have called them Presbyterians, because most of them object to being designated by the name of Calvinists.[99]

The Menonists,[100] the Moravians,[101] the Swin-

[97] The so-called Union Churches of eastern Pennsylvania, some of which have persisted to this day. They are not "Union" in the modern sense of that term. They are two separate congregations, with separate pastors, separate worship and separate literature, but they unite in the building of one church edifice, occupied alternately by pastors of each denomination, and with portions of both congregations attending all services.

[98] The *Heidelberg Catechism,* the symbolical book adopted by the German Reformed church, is, in its general character, Calvinistic. This formulary observes a singular moderation on some points, upon which the several parties in the Protestant churches differed, or respecting which good men might entertain different opinions. The Heidelberg Catechism is more irenical than otherwise.—I. D. Rupp.

[99] This sentence is omitted in the text of Rupp.

[100] Ely, *Kurzgefasste Kirchen-Geschichte der Menoniten,* n. d., Lancaster, Pa.; Musser, *The Reformed Mennonite Church,* Lancaster, Pa., 1878; Wedel, *Geschichte der Mennoniten,* 4 vols., Newton, Kans., 1900–1902; Smith, *The Mennonites of America,* Goshen, Ind., 1909. See also Horsch in *New Sch.-Herzog,* VII., 1910.

gelders,[102] and the Catholics, compose the other sects of the German inhabitants of Pennsylvania. The Menonists hold war and oaths to be unlawful. They admit the sacraments of baptism by sprinkling,[103] and the supper. From them [104] a sect has arisen, who hold, with the above principles and ceremonies, the necessity of immersion baptism; hence they are called Dunkers,[105] or Baptists. Previously to their partaking of the sacrament of the supper, they wash each other's feet, and sit down to a love-feast. They practice these ceremonies of their religion with great humility and solemnity. They, moreover, hold the doctrine of universal sal-

---

[101] Reichel, *Early History of the Church of the United Brethren;* De Schweinitz, *Moravian Settlements in Pennsylvania, Proceedings of the Pennsylvania-German Society,* IV., 53; Levering, *A History of Bethlehem, Pennsylvania, 1741–1892,* Bethlehem, 1903.

[102] See Kriebel, *The Schwenkfelders, Proceedings of the Pennsylvania-German Society,* XIII., pp. 1–225.

[103] The Mennonites baptize the subject while kneeling, by pouring water upon the head of the person being baptized.—I. D. Rupp.

[104] Dr. Rush's statement lacks historical proof. The Dunkers (German Brethren), as a sect, have not arisen from the Mennonites. Alexander Mack, of Vitchengestein, of Prussia, founded, 1708, this sect. Rev. Peter Becker, one of the German Brethren ministers came to Pennsylvania, 1719. Alexander Mack followed Becker to Pennsylvania, 1729, settled near Germantown—died 1735, aged 65—buried in Brethren burying ground, at Germantown.—I. D. Rupp.

[105] See Falkenstein, *The German Baptist Brethren or Dunkards, Proceedings of the Pennsylvania-German Society,* X.

vation. From this sect there have been several seceders, one of whom devoted himself to perpetual celibacy.[106] They have exhibited for many years, a curious spectacle of pious mortification, at a village called Ephrata,[107] in Lancaster County. They are at present reduced to fourteen or fifteen members. The Separatists who likewise dissented from the Dunkers, reject the ordinance of baptism and the sacrament; and hold the doctrine of the Friends, concerning the internal revelation of the gospel. They hold, with the Dunkers, the doctrine of universal salvation.[108] The singular piety, and exemplary morality of these sects,[109] have been urged, by the advocates for the salvation of all mankind, as a proof that the belief of that doctrine is not so unfriendly to morals, and the order of society, as has been supposed. The Dunkers and Separatists agree in taking no interest upon money, and in not applying to law to recover their debts.

The German Moravians are a numerous and respectable body of christians in Pennsylvania. In their village of Bethlehem, there are two large stone buildings, in which the different sexes are educated in habits of industry in useful manufac-

---

[106] Conrad Beissel.

[107] For the Community at Ephrata, and many others of the early religionists, see Sachse, *The German Sectarians of Pennsylvania, 1708–1742*, two volumes, Philadelphia, 1899.

[108] This last clause must be received *cum grano salis.*—I. D. Rupp.

[109] See Sachse, *The German Sectarians.*

tures. The sisters (for by that epithet the women are called) all sleep in two large and neat apartments. Two of them watch over the rest, in turns, every night, to afford relief from the sudden indispositions which sometimes occur, in the most healthy persons, in the hours of sleep. It is impossible to record this fact, without pausing a moment to do homage to that religion, which produces so much union and kindness in human souls. The number of women, who belong to this sequestered female society, amounts sometimes to 120, and seldom to less than 100. It is remarkable that notwithstanding they lead a sedentary life, and sit constantly in close stove rooms in winter, that not more than one of them, upon an average, dies in a year. The disease which generally produces this annual death, is the consumption. The conditions and ages of the women of the village, as well as of the society that has been mentioned, are distinguished by ribbons of a peculiar kind which they wear on their caps; the widows, by white; the married women, by blue; the single women, above 18 years of age, by pink; and those under that age, by a ribbon of a cinnamon colour. Formerly this body of Moravians held all their property in common in imitation of the primitive christians; but, in the year 1760, a division of the whole of it took place, except a tavern,[110] a tan-yard, 2000

[110] *The Old Sun Inn,* Reichel, *Proceedings of the Pennsylvania-German Society,* VI., pp. 44–74.

acres of land near Bethlehem, and 5000 acres near Nazareth, a village in the neighborhood of Bethlehem. The profits of these estates are appropriated to the support and propagation of the gospel. There are many valuable manufactures[111] carried on at Bethlehem. The inhabitants possess a gentleness in their manners, which is peculiarly agreeable to strangers. They inure their children, of five and six years old, to habits of early industry. By this means they are not only taught those kinds of labour which are suited to their strength and capacity, but are preserved from many of the hurtful vices and accidents to which children are exposed.[112]

The Swingfelders are a small society.[113] They

---

[111] See, *e. g., The Pottery of the Pennsylvania-Germans* by Henry C. Mercer, *The Pennsylvania-German,* April, 1901.

[112] The Moravians, by reason of their deep interest in Pennsylvania-German history, of the vast quantities of intelligent and reliable historical material contained in the diaries of the pastors of their congregations, from the early dates down, of the large store of historical documents to be found in their archives at Bethlehem, and because of their cemeteries, their interests in education, and their quaint and well-preserved historical buildings, are among the most valuable contributors to researches in Pennsylvania-German history.

[113] *Corpus Schwenckfeldianorum,* Vol. I. Dr. Chester D. Hartranft, Hartford Theological Seminary, editor-in-chief; Otto Bernhard Schlutter, Hartford Theological Seminary; Rev. E. E. S. Johnson, Hartford Theological Seminary, associate editors. LXX., 661 pp. Breitkopf & Härtel, Leipzig, 1907. The first volume of a complete edition of the writings of Caspar Schwenckfeld, undertaken by the Schwenckfelders in America.

Neu-Eingerichtetes
Gesang-Buch
in sich haltend
eine
Sammlung
(mehrentheils alter)
schöner lehr-reicher und erbaulicher
Lieder,
Welche von langer Zeit her bey den Bekennern
und Liebhabern der Glorien und Wahrheits
Jesu Christi bis anietzo in Übung
gewesen.
Nach den Haupt-Stücken der Christlichen Lehr und Glaubens eingetheilet,
und
Mit einem Verzeichniß der Titel
und dreyen Nützlichen Registern
versehen
Anjetzo also zusammen getragen,
und
Zum Lobe GOttes und heilsamen
Erbauung im Christenthum,
ans Licht gegeben.

Germantown, gedruckt bey Christoph Saur,
auf Kosten etlicher Freunden. 1762

Singen das löblichste Geschäfte.

Hör, Seel! jetzt sollt du rathen
Was unter allen Thaten
Am besten sey zu thun?
Schau! was thun denn die droben,
Die dein Herr selbst erheben,
Zu dienen stets vor seinem Thron
Weil dort der Engel Schaaren
Mit tausend tausend Paaren
Den schönsten Lobgesang
Vor Gottes Throne führen
Dem Lamme jubiliren,
Mit allersüßtem Musik-Klang.

Neueingerichtetes
Gesang-Buch,
enthaltend eine
Sammlung
(mehrentheils alter)
erbaulicher Lieder,
nach den Hauptstücken der Christlichen Lehre und
Glaubens eingetheilet.

Philadelphia:
Gedruckt bey Conrad Zentler, in der Zweyten Straße,
unterhalb der Rehs-Straße.
1813.

Neueingerichtetes
Gesang-Buch,
enthaltend
eine Sammlung erbaulicher Lieder,
nach den Haupt-Stücken
christlicher Lehre.
Herausgegeben auf Verordnung
der
Schwenkfelder Gemeinde.

Druck von D. G. Dambly, Skippackville, Pa.
1869

A Group of Pennsylvania-German Hymn Books (Schwenkfeldian). "They hold the same principles as the Friends, but they differ from them in using psalmody in their worship."

hold the same principles as the Friends, but they differ from them in using psalmody in their worship.

The German Catholics[114] are numerous in Philadelphia and have several small chapels in other parts of the state.

There is an incorporated charitable society of Germans[115] in Philadelphia, whose objects are their poor and distressed countrymen.

(See somewhat extended review of the work in The Pennsylvania-German of March, 1908, by Prof. E. S. Gerhard, Trenton, N. J.)

[114] Kirlin, *Catholicity in Philadelphia;* Lambing, *History of the Catholic Church in the Dioceses of Pittsburg and Allegheny.* See also *Records of the American Catholic Historical Society* and the *American Catholic Historical Researches.*

[115] The German Society of Philadelphia, in the Province of Pennsylvania, was incorporated 1764. This society supplied the poor, the sick and otherwise distressed Germans; . . . to teach and improve their poor children, both in English and German languages, reading and writing thereof, and to procure for them such learning and education, as would best suit their genius and capacities, and enable the proper objects to receive the finishing of their studies in the University of Philadelphia; likewise to erect a library, etc.

The officers of the society, named in the act of incorporation were: Henry Keppele, *President;* Lewis Weiss, *Vice-President;* Lewis Farmer and Henry Leuthaeuser, *Secretaries;* Christoph Ludwig, Peter Ozeas, Andrew Burkhard, John Fritz, Peter Kraft and Melchior Steiner, *Overseers;* Michael Schubert, *Treasurer;* Henry Kaemmerer, *Solicitor;* William Lehman, *Deacon.*—I. D. Rupp.

This Society is still in existence, and has just unveiled a monument in City Hall Square to the memory of General Peter Muhlenberg.

There is likewise a German society of labourers; and journeymen mechanics, who contribute 2s. 6d. eight times a year, towards a fund, out of which they allow 30d. a week to each other's families, when the head of it is unable to work; and 7l.10s. to his widow, as soon as he is taken from his family by death.[115a]

[115a] The grandfather of the present writer was for many years the secretary of the Unterstuetzungs-Verein of the St. Michaels, Zions and St. Pauls German Lutheran congregations, Philadelphia, conducted on somewhat similar principles.

CULTURE AND PROSPERITY.

THE Germans of Pennsylvania, including all the sects that have been mentioned, compose nearly one third part[116] of the whole inhabitants of the state.

The intercourse of the Germans with each other, is kept up chiefly in their own language;[117] but most of their men, who visit the capital, and the trading or country towns of the state, speak the English language. A certain number of

[116] See other estimates in The Introduction to this "Account."

[117] This is still the case in 1910, one hundred and thirty years after Dr. Rush wrote his "Account." The hearty, personal, simple, unconventional character of the German language, and particularly of the Pennsylvania-German dialect, causes it to retain its hold on the minds of the people; and, although the dialect is dying out, German services are well attended in many churches in the country, and the German Scripture and German sermon are preferred because of the simplicity and superior heart power of Luther's translation to the more abstract language of the English version, by those who are masters of both tongues, but who were brought up by German parents.

the laws of the state are now printed in German, for the benefit of those of them who cannot read English. A large number of German newspapers[118] are likewise circulated through the state, through which knowledge and intelligence have been conveyed, much to the advantage of the government. There is scarcely an instance of a German, of either sex, in Pennsylvania, that cannot read; but many of the wives and daughters of the German farmers cannot write. The present state of society among them renders this accomplishment of little consequence to their improvement or happiness.

If it were possible to determine the amount of all the property brought into Pennsylvania by the present German inhabitants of the state, and their ancestors, and then compare it with the present amount of their property, the contrast would form such a monument of human industry and economy as has seldom been contemplated in any age or country.[118a]

---

118 Philadelphia still supports German newspapers, but the real Pennsylvania-German newspapers of the inland cities and towns have died out. In the city of the writer, its line of German weeklies, after a continuous existence of over a century, ceased less than three years ago. The free rural delivery which brings the daily paper of the metropolis to the farmer's home every twenty-four hours is one of the potent causes of this decline.

118a "Dr. Rush says the Pennsylvania farms produced millions of dollars, which after 1780 made possible the foundation of the Bank of North America (chartered 1781)."—Faust, *The German Element in the United States*, I., p. 139.

I have been informed that there was an ancient prophecy which foretold, that "God would bless the Germans in foreign countries." This prediction has been faithfully verified in Pennsylvania. They enjoy here every blessing that liberty, toleration, independence, affluence, virtue and reputation, can confer upon them.

How different is their situation here; from what it was in Germany! Could the subjects of the princes of Germany, who now groan away their lives in slavery and unprofitable labour, view from an eminence, in the month of June, the German settlements of Stratsburg, or Manheim in Lancaster[119] county, or of Lebanon or Bethlehem[120] in the counties of Dauphin and Northampton; could they be accompanied on this eminence, by a venerable German farmer, and be told by him that many of those extensive fields of grain, full-fed herds, luxuriant meadows, orchards, promising loads of fruit, together with the spacious barns—and commodious stone-dwelling houses, which compose the prospects that have been mentioned, were all the product of the labour of a single family, and of one genera-

[119] See *Proceedings of the Lancaster County Historical Society.*

[120] See *Proceedings of the Lebanon County Historical Society;* also Schmauk, *Old Salem in Lebanon, a History of the Congregation and Town,* Lebanon, Pa., 1898; Croll, *Ancient and Historic Landmarks of the Lebanon Valley,* Philadelphia, Pa., 1895. For Dauphin County see Egle, *History of the Counties of Dauphin and Lebanon,* Philadelphia, 1883. For Bethlehem, see work by Bishop Levering referred to above.

tion; and that they were all secured to the owners of them by certain laws; I am persuaded, that no chains would be able to detain them from sharing in the freedom of their Pennsylvania friends and former fellow-subjects. "We will assert our dignity—(would be their language) we will be men—we will be free—we will enjoy the fruits of our own labours—we will no longer be bought and sold to fight battles[121]—in which we have neither interest nor resentment—we will inherit a portion of that blessing which God has promised to the Germans in foreign countries—we will be Pennsylvanians."

I shall conclude this account of the manners of

---

[121] Germans had been sold by their lords to England, to fight battles in which they had no interest, at several periods—1702, 1726, 1743, 1745. In the *prosopopœia: "we will no longer be bought and sold,"* are personated collectively Germans, called *Huelfs truppen,* subsidiary-troops, sold by several German dukes, landgraves, margraves, to the King of England, 1776–1783, to wage an exterminating war against the American colonies. The Duke of Brunswick sold 5,733; the Prince of Hanau, 2,422; the Margrave of Anspach, 1,644; the Prince of Waldeck, 1,225; the Prince of Anhalt Zerbst, 1,160; the Landgrave of Hesse Cassel, 1,200; the Hereditary Prince of Hesse Cassel, 796; the Margrave of Brandenberg, 1,200—besides others. The aggregate number of these Germans that *perished in battle,* exceeded upwards of *eleven thousand.*

The sale of these subjects was a profitable business to their *humane lords.* The sum total paid by His Britannic Majesty to the several princes and dukes, was $8,100,000.—I. D. Rupp.

It should be remembered that the kings of England at this time were themselves German princes.

the German inhabitants of Pennsylvania by remarking that if I have failed in doing them justice,[122] it has not been the fault of my subject. The German character once employed the pen of the first historians of antiquity. I mean the elegant and enlightened Tacitus.[123] It is very remarkable that the Germans in Pennsylvania retain in a great degree all the virtues,[123a] which this author ascribes to their ancestors in his treatise " de moribus

---

[122] If all other writers on the subject, including many later ones, had done the Pennsylvania-Germans anything like the substantial justice which has been accorded them by the keen observation and clear judgment of the author of this "Account," their position in American literature to-day would be different from what it actually is.

[123] Dr. Rush was a keen observer, and possessed a judicial mind. He noticed that the prosperity of Pennsylvania was largely due to the Pennsylvania-Germans and began to examine into the causes of their success. He seems consciously to have imitated the example of the historian Tacitus, who described the virtues and vices of the ancient Germans, perhaps with a view to holding them up as an example for his own people.—Faust, *The German Element in the United States,* 1909, p. 130.

[123a] While a Pennsylvania-German reared to the high qualities of his ancestral stock does deserve the encomium here given, on the other hand, a degenerate Pennsylvania-German is perhaps the worst of all the specimens of a ruined humanity. Boldness, rudeness, vulgarity, coarse sensuality, idleness, utter disregard of financial responsibility, and, in general, the lack of even those outer forms of culture which serve as a restraint in the public eye, frequently mark a degenerate and abandoned Pennsylvania stock, such as are to be found on the streets of our inland towns. Several of the most flourishing of these inland cities, and numerous

Germanorum."—They inherit their integrity—fidelity—and chastity[124]—but Christianity has banished from them, their drunkenness, idleness, and love of military glory. There is a singular trait in the features of the German character in Pennsylvania, which shews how long the most trifling customs may exist among a people who have not been mixed with other nations. Tacitus describes the manner in which the ancient Germans build their villages in the following words. "Suam quisque domum spatiis circumdat sive adversus casus ignis remedium, sive inscitia edificandi."[124a] Many of the German villages in Pennsylvania are constructed in the same manner. The small houses are composed of a mixture, of wood, brick and clay, neatly united together. The large houses built of stone, and many of them after the English fashion. Very few of the houses in Germantown are connected together. Where the Germans connect their houses in their villages, they appear to have deviated from one of the customs they imported from Germany.

---

smaller manufacturing hamlets have become notorious because of the depraved life and wickedness which has been engrafted on parts of the originally noble and substantial Pennsylvania-German stock.

[124] Severe illic matrimonia: nec ullam morem partem magis laudaveris: The matrimonial bond is strict and severe among them; nor is there anything in their manners more commendable than this.—I. D. Rupp.

[124a] Each man leaves a space between his house, and those of his neighbors, either to avoid the danger from fire, or from unskilfulness in architecture.

THE CONCLUSION.

CITIZENS of the United States learn from the account that has been given of the German inhabitants of Pennsylvania, to prize knowledge and industry in agriculture[125] and manufactures,[126] as the basis of domestic happiness and national prosperity.

[125] These words of Dr. Rush sound very much like the most modern utterances of James J. Hill, the western railroad king, on agriculture.

[126] Little did Dr. Rush dream that the Keystone State, as it has been now called, would become the great manufacturing state of the Union. Although the first iron furnace in Pittsburg was built in 1792 by George Anshutz, pig iron was not again made in Pittsburg until 1859, and the whole manufacturing development of the western part of the state, and the corresponding development to be found in such eastern parts of the state as Bethlehem, are quite recent in their growth; while the problem of immigration has shifted from that of the Germanic, to that of the Slav and the Romance nations.

LEGISLATORS of the United States, learn from the wealth and independence of the German inhabitants of Pennsylvania, to encourage by your example, and laws, the republican virtues of industry and economy. They are the only pillars which can support the present constitution of the United States.[127]

THE PENNSYLVANIA-GERMAN IN THE REVOLUTIONARY WAR.

[127] In note 78 we have stated that Dr. Rush does not directly mention the valuable services of the Pennsylvania-Germans in the Revolutionary War. He may not have deemed it advisable to stir up old memories in the hearts of those to whom he was writing, as this would interfere with his commendation of the Germans to a portion of the English in Pennsylvania. His own memories and sufferings in the War of the Revolution may have deterred him from alluding to it, and the period in which he was now writing was that in which the thought of reconstruction, and not of warfare was uppermost, and he therefore emphasizes the virtues of the Germans with reference to this first constitutional period. But we have deemed it proper, especially since brief summaries of the service of German eastern Pennsylvania to the Revolution are not so accessible, to present a note on that subject:

During the Revolutionary War almost the entire frontier from Maine to Georgia was occupied by the German immigrants and their descendants. Nearly one-half of the whole number, estimated by some at 110,000 souls, were located in Pennsylvania. The same estimate sets the Germans in New York at 25,000, in Virginia and West Virginia at 25,000, in Maryland and Delaware at 20,500, in New Jersey at 15,000, in South Carolina at 15,000, in North Carolina at 8,000, in Georgia at 5,000, and in New England at 1,500. The Pennsylvania-German riflemen, the best marksmen in the American army, and the terror of the British, were a powerful factor, at the siege of Boston, in the defense of New York, and saved the army of Washington from annihilation in the battle of

LEGISLATORS of Pennsylvania,—learn from the history of your German fellow citizens that you

---

Long Island. As Captain H. M. M. Richards says, "They turned the tide at Saratoga by their sharp shooting, they were Morgan's reliance at Cowpens." (See Heckman, *The Battle of Long Island, Proceedings of the Pennsylvania-German Society,* III.; Heller, *Gun Makers of Old Northampton, Proceedings of the Pennsylvania-German Society,* XVII.; Richards, *The Pennsylvania-Germans in the Revolutionary War, Proceedings of the Pennsylvania-German Society,* XVII.)

The Germans in Pennsylvania formed a solid background for the whole war. Their farms were the granary of the colonies. Their leaders were patriots in word and deed. Rev. Michael Schlatter was the chaplain of a regiment during the Revolution. Rev. Henry Melchior Muhlenberg, through his sons and through his congregation, fostered the cause of independence. Such representative men as Ludwick, Schlosser, Engel, Hillegas, Hubley, Barge, Rosz, Ferree, Slough, Erwin, Schultz, Potts, Küchlein, Arndt, Weitzel, Hasenclever, Melcher, Wagner, Graf, Kuhn, Eichelberger, Smeiser, Levan, and Gehr, met as early as 1774 in Philadelphia to support the position taken by Massachusetts; and in the middle of June sent offers of men and money to Boston.

In 1775 the vestries of the German Lutheran and Reformed churches in Philadelphia issued a pamphlet of forty pages for the Germans of New York and North Carolina, in which they set forth the fact that the Germans in all parts of Pennsylvania had formed militia companies together with a select corps of sharpshooters, while those unable to do military service were willing to furnish contributions. This broadside was an earnest appeal to the Germans in other colonies for armed resistance against the English government. Bancroft (*History of the United States of America from the Discovery of the Continent,* IV., p. 318) says: "In the valley of the Blue Ridge the German congregations, quickened by the preaching of Muhlenberg, were eager to take up arms." The German Society of Philadelphia was active in the cause.

possess an inexhaustible treasure in the bosom of the state, in their manners and arts. Continue to

On June 14, 1775, three days before the battle of Bunker Hill, and a day before the appointment of Washington as commander-in-chief, Congress authorized the raising of six companies of expert riflemen in Pennsylvania, two in Maryland, and two in Virginia. On June 22d, Pennsylvania was directed to raise two more companies. The first company to go from Pennsylvania to Boston was Captain Nagle's Pennsylvania-Germans from Berks County. These Reading riflemen had marched to Boston by July 18th, thirty-four days after Congress had authorized the formation of the battalion. In less than another month the power of their rifles and the accuracy of their aim were known to both the British and the American forces, neither of whom had seen a rifle before.

At the battle of Long Island, Colonel Miles with his Pennsylvania Rifle Regiment formed the extreme left, with Colonel Atlee's Pennsylvania Musketry Battalion on the right center, and Lutz's Battalion supporting them. The Germans were barely of 5,000, with the British of 20,000 against them. These riflemen, with the enemy on front, in the flank, and in the rear, died to save the American army. Colonel Küchlein's company from Easton went into battle with less than a hundred men, and came out with seventy-one of them dead. Thompson's Rifle Battalion was one of the finest organizations in the Continental Army, and was Pennsylvania-German, largely from Lancaster and York counties. Two-thirds of Morgan's "Virginians," a picked corps of rifle sharpshooters, were Pennsylvanians, and a large part of them Pennsylvania-Germans. With von Ottendorff's corps and Schott's dragoons, and Pulaski's Legion, they did gallant service in the south and at Yorktown. Pulaski's Legion carried an embroidered crimson standard made by the Moravian single sisters of Bethlehem.

When it was suspected that there were Tories in the bodyguard of Washington, its personnel was changed, and the leaders turned to the trusty Germans, of whom it was now made up. Van

patronize their newly established seminary of learn-

Heer's independent Troop of Horse, recruited chiefly in Berks and Lancaster counties, was composed entirely of Germans, who entered the war in the spring of 1778, and were honorably discharged at the end of the war. Twelve of them, who had served longer than any other American soldiers, escorted Washington to his home at Mount Vernon at the close of the war. Hundreds of German soldiers served in the continental regiments 1 to 13 of Pennsylvania. The First Pennsylvania Battalion, commanded by Colonel John Philip de Haas, a Pennsylvania-German from Lebanon, took part in the Canada expedition of General Arnold. The Second Pennsylvania Battalion was almost entirely Pennsylvania-German and also went to Canada, in part under the leadership of Colonels Wayne and Allen. The Third and Fifth Pennsylvania Battalions were largely Pennsylvania-German. Miles' Rifle Regiment was made up of Pennsylvania-Germans.

John Peter Muhlenberg was the right hand man of Baron Steuben, in Virginia, in creating an army, and won distinction at the battles of Charleston, Brandywine, Germantown, Monmouth, Stony Point and Yorktown. His regiment was always better filled than others. At the Brandywine, his brigade covered the retreat of the American army and prevented its annihilation by Cornwallis. At Germantown it divided the wing of the enemy in a brilliant bayonet attack. Steuben's influence, by which he transformed the Revolutionary Army into a well disciplined body, was altogether German. His brigade was at least one-half German, and was in the trenches at Yorktown, when the first overtures of peace came from Cornwallis. The Continental Army contained many Pennsylvania-German officers, among whom were General Daniel Hiester, Colonel Frederick Antes, Lieutenant Colonel Jacob Reed, Captain John Hiester, Captain John Arndt, Colonel Peter Küchlein, Colonel Philip Greenawalt, Colonel Nicholas Hausegger and many others. David Ziegler, of Lancaster, as the adjutant of the second Pennsylvania regiment to enlist for the war under Washington, became the senior captain of the First Pennsylvania Conti-

ing and spare no expense[128] in supporting their public free-schools. The vices which follow the want of religious instruction,[129] among the children

nental Regiment. Daniel Hiester, of Reading, had four sons, all of whom entered the army as officers. Joseph Hiester became brigadier general on Washington's recommendation. Among the German officers that fell were Lieutenant Colonel Küchlein, Piper, and Lutz. (See H. M. M. Richards, *The Pennsylvania-German in the Revolutionary War, Proceedings of the Pennsylvania-German Society,* XVII.; Rosengarten, *German Soldiers in the War of the United States,* Philadelphia, 1890; Faust, *The German Element in the United States,* Houghton Mifflin & Co., 1909.)

[128] Pennsylvania appropriates annually five million dollars for the cause of education. The state system of education, from its introduction under the German governors, and from the days of Higbee and Wickersham down to the present moment, except the University of Pennsylvania, is in control of Pennsylvania-German educators. The Superintendent of Public Instruction in the State, Dr. N. C. Schaeffer, and the Superintendent of Public Schools in Philadelphia, Dr. Martin Brumbaugh, are both Pennsylvania-Germans.

[129] As we have seen, Dr. Rush was deeply interested in public education, especially in the education of the lower classes, and he found a man after his own heart in the person of the German Christopher Ludwick. Ludwick devised the bulk of his estate for the public education of the poor, and there are certain indications from which it may perhaps be inferred that this disposition was suggested to him by Dr. Rush, or that Dr. Rush, at least, aided him in putting his desire into proper form. In his account of the life of Ludwick, Rush devotes much space to recounting the terms of this legacy as follows:

"The same just and charitable disposition which governed his actions in life, manifested itself in an eminent degree in his will;

of poor people, lay the foundation of most of the jails, and places of public punishment in the state.

in which after bequeathing various family legacies, he gives five hundred pounds, in equal shares, to the German Reformed Church in Philadelphia, to the German Society, to the University of Pennsylvania, and the Lutheran Church at Beggarstown, to be employed in educating poor children. To the Pennsylvania Hospital, he gives one hundred pounds for the relief of poor patients, and to the Guardians of the Poor, two hundred pounds, to be laid out in fire wood for the use of the poor in Philadelphia. The residue of his estate is then disposed of by the following bequest, viz.:

"'Item. As I have, ever since I arrived to the years of discretion, seen the benefit and advantage that arise to the community by the education and instruction of poor children, and have earnestly desired that an institution could be established in this city or liberties, for the education of poor children of all denominations gratis, without any exception to country, extraction or religious principles of their friends or parents; and as the residue and remainder of my estate will, in my opinion, amount to upwards of three thousand pounds specie, I am willing that the same shall be my mite or contribution towards such institution, and flatter myself that many others will add and contribute to the fund for so laudable a purpose. And therefore I do will, devise, and direct that all the residue and remainder of my estate, real and personal, whatsoever and wheresoever, not hereinbefore otherwise disposed of, shall be appropriated as and towards a fund, for the schooling and educating gratis, of poor children of all denominations, in the city and liberties of Philadelphia, without any exception to the country, extraction, or religious principles of their parents or friends; and for that purpose shall be vested by my executors, or the survivers or surviver of them, or the executor of such surviver, in the public funds, or placed out at interest on good and sufficient land security, or in the purchase of well-secured ground rents, and the annual interest and

Do not contend with their prejudices in favour of their language. It will be the channel through

---

income thereof, from time to time, used and applied by them my said executors and the survivers or surviver of them, and in case of all their deaths, then by the Guardians or Overseers of the Poor in the said city or liberties for the time being, and their successors, for the sole use and purpose of defraying the expense of schooling and educating of such poor children of the said city or liberties, whose parents or friends cannot afford to pay for the same, without any exception as above mentioned, until an institution and free school on the liberal principles as herein above mentioned, shall be established and incorporated in the said city or liberties, when all the said residue and remainder of my estate, whether in stock, mortgages or ground rents, and otherwise, shall vest in and be added to the fund of such charitable institution and free school, for the use and purpose of educating poor children as above mentioned forever.'

"If before the lapse of five years, such a school should not be established, he orders the said residue of his estate, to be divided in unequal shares among the German Lutheran, the German Reformed, the English Episcopal, the First and Second Presbyterian, the Roman Catholic, and the African Churches, and the University of Pennsylvania, to be employed by them, exclusively in educating poor children."—Rush, *Life of Christopher Ludwick,* pp. 23–26.

Dr. Rush regarded Ludwick himself as a striking illustration of the benefit of free schools. He says: "Without the advantages Mr. Ludwick derived from one of them, he might have passed through life in obscurity, or ended his days prematurely, from the operation of vices which are the results of a defect of education. It was from a grateful sense of the usefulness of the knowledge he acquired in a free school, that he took so much pains during his life, and in his will, to render that degree of knowledge more general, by educating the children of the poor people."—Rush, *Life of Christopher Ludwick,* pp. 27, 28.

which the knowledge and discoveries of one of the wisest nations in Europe, may be conveyed into our country.[130] In proportion as they are instructed and enlightened in their own language, they will become acquainted with the language of the United States. Invite them to share in the power and offices of government;[131] it will be the means of

"He died in June 1801, leaving his residuary estate, estimated then at eight thousand dollars, to the association which should be first incorporated, for the purpose of teaching gratis, poor children in the city or liberties of Philadelphia, without any exception to the country, extraction or religion of their parents or friends. The magnitude of the bequest excited a desire in the then trustees of the University of Pennsylvania, to become the managers of this fund, and they of course became competitors with the society, in the endeavour to be first to obtain a charter."—Rush, *Life of Christopher Ludwick*, pp. 36, 37.

[130] A prophecy which has been most remarkably fulfilled, *e. g.*, by the writings of Prof. Hugo Münsterberg, of Harvard.

See Hinsdale, *Notes on the History of Foreign Influence upon Education in the United States, Report of the Commissioner of Education,* 1897–1898, Vol. I., pp. 604–607, and Learned, *Dedication of the Bechstein Library in Philadelphia,* March 21, 1896.

[131] THE GERMAN GOVERNORS OF PENNSYLVANIA.

Here, again, the prophetic exhortation of Dr. Rush has been most remarkably fulfilled: "Politically the Germans long took an important part in Pennsylvania, all the governors of the State from 1808 to 1838 with one exception being of German origin."—Barr Ferree, *Pennsylvania: A Primer,* 1904, p. 102. The first German governor, Snyder, was a member of the Constitutional Convention of 1789, a member of the House of Representatives for ten years, and Speaker of the House for the last

producing an union in principle and conduct between them, and those of their enlightened fellow citizens who are descended from other nations. Above all, cherish with peculiar tenderness, those sects among them who hold war to be unlawful.—Relieve them from the oppression of absurd and unnecessary militia laws. Protect them as the repositories of a truth of the gospel, which has existed in every age of the church, and which must spread hereafter over every part of the world.

---

six years of his congressional life. His gubernatorial administration covered the period of the War of 1812. Governor Hiester had a brilliant Revolutionary record, was a member of the Convention to Ratify the National Constitution, and represented Berks District in Congress for fourteen years. His term began in 1820. Governor John Andrew Schultze was a German Lutheran clergyman, born in Berks County, and represented Lebanon and Dauphin counties in the State Senate. He was elected Governor by the largest proportionate popular majority ever given a gubernatorial candidate in the State. He filled two terms. Governor Wolf was a German of Easton, and a member of Congress. Under him the common school system was established throughout the state. Governor Ritner was the son of an Alsatian immigrant, practically without any schooling. He was Speaker of the State Legislature, and put the common school law into practical operation. Governor Porter was born in Montgomery County and was chosen for two terms. Governor Schunk, born at the Trappe, was chief clerk of the House of Representatives. His administration included the Mexican War. The colonial records in the Pennsylvania archives were begun during his administration. Governor Bigler, Governor Hartranft, Governor Beaver, and Governor Pennypacker were all of the blood of whom Dr. Rush said, " Invite them to share in the offices of government."

The opinions respecting the commerce and slavery of the Africans, which have nearly produced a revolution in their favour, in some of the European governments, were transplanted from a sect of christians in Pennsylvania.[132] Perhaps those German Sects of christians among us, who refuse to bear arms for the purpose of shedding human blood, may be preserved by divine providence, as the centre of a circle, which shall gradually embrace all the nations of the earth in a perpetual treaty of friendship and peace.[133]

---

[132] In March, 1780, the first abolition act passed in America was adopted by the Pennsylvania Assembly. It provided a gradual decrease which reduced the numbers from four thousand slaves at that date to two hundred in 1820. In 1794 a convention of abolition societies was held in Philadelphia. The Wilmot Proviso was offered by a Pennsylvanian in 1846 and declared that neither slavery nor involuntary servitude shall ever exist in any new territory acquired by the United States. Barr Ferree declares that the history of Pennsylvania "shows a more consistent and longer sustained condemnation of slavery than does that of any other state." Abraham Lincoln himself was the descendant of a Pennsylvania immigrant who lived in Berks County, so that Dr. Rush's own views and efforts in this direction were wonderfully fulfilled by the State whose legislators he is here addressing.

[133] Within the last ten years, the closing desire of Dr. Rush, in connection with his account of the qualities of men of German blood, viz., that there may be "a circle, which shall gradually embrace all the nations of the earth in a perpetual treaty of friendship and peace," has been making some progress toward fulfillment. The establishment of the Peace Conference at the Hague in 1899, at first deemed so visionary (see *The Peace Conference at the Hague and its Bearing on International Law*

and Abolition, by Frederick W. Holls, D.D., C. L. Macmillan, New York, 1900) has at least become a matter of history, and the words of its first President M. de Staal, have impressed themselves upon many rulers: "The nations have a great need for peace, and we owe it to humanity—we owe it to the governments which have given us their powers and who are responsible for the good of their peoples—we owe it to ourselves to accomplish a useful work in finding the method of employing some of the means for the purpose of insuring peace. It is to this high labor that we must concentrate our efforts—sustained by the conviction that we are laboring for the good of all humanity, according to the way which preceding generations have foreseen."—Holls, pp. 61, 62.

One of the leading members of this conference from America, and the author who has given us the story of its workings in print, the particular friend of Theodore Roosevelt, was the son of a German clergyman in Pennsylvania. And now that the policy of Mr. Roosevelt and of the German Emperor, which seems to be that of ultimate peace, on a basis of righteousness, has just been made prominent throughout Europe, and Mr. Taft's Pennsylvania Secretary of State, Mr. Knox, has declared it as his view that the era of universal international arbitration will be at hand before many years have elapsed, the thought of Dr. Rush, after coursing its way through blood, shed by our nation, righteously and unrighteously, for over a century, proves itself to be the predominant aspiration of leading American public minds of the Twentieth Century.

THE END

INDEX TO SUBJECTS.

INDEX TO PROPER NAMES.

SURGEON'S HALL, FIFTH STREET, EAST SIDE, BELOW LIBRARY STREET.

BUILT 1765, DEMOLISHED 1802.

ORIGINAL IN COLLECTION OF JULIUS F. SACHSE.

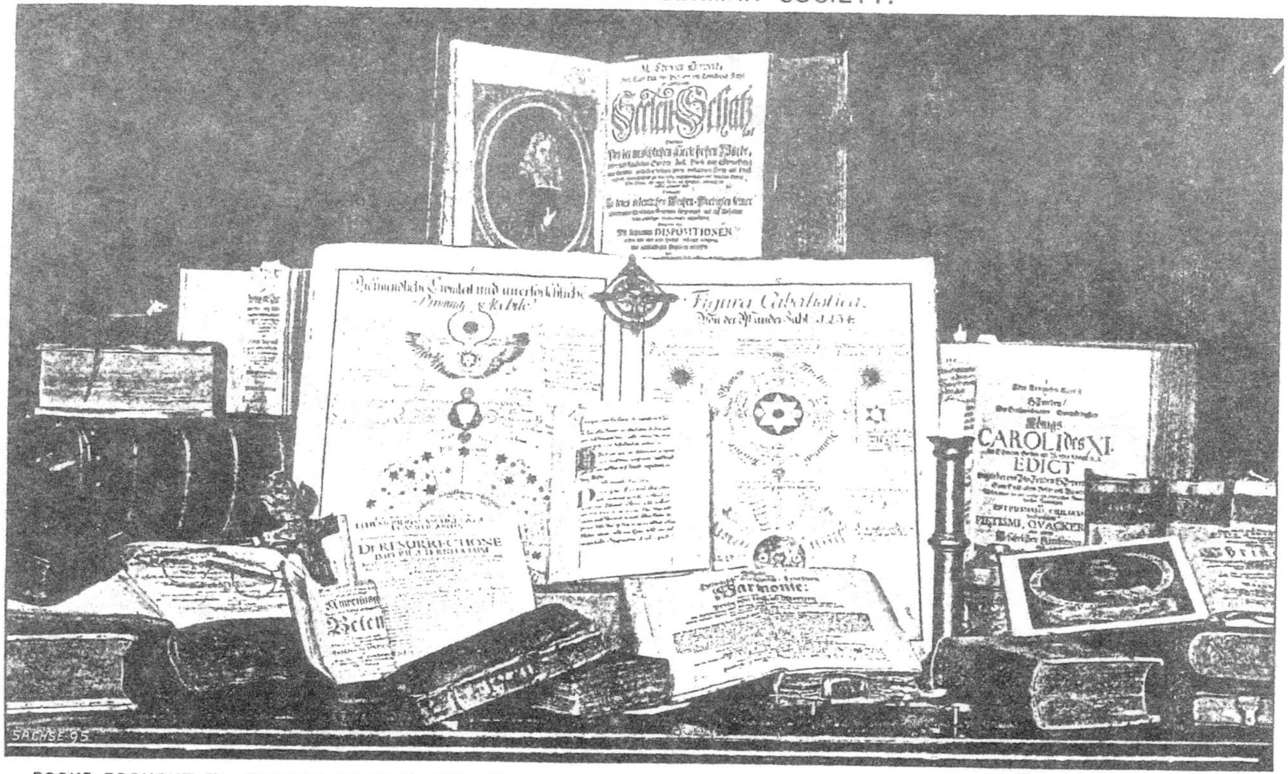

BOOKS BROUGHT TO AMERICA BY THE GERMAN PIETISTS CONTEMPORARY WITH WILLIAM PENN, AND ILLUSTRATING THE LEARNING AND LITERARY CULTURE OF THE EARLY PENNSYLVANIA GERMANS.

IN POSSESSION OF JULIUS F. SACHSE, LITT. D.

PENNSYLVANIA-GERMAN LAMPS AND TINWARE, XVIII CENTURY.

HOUSE INSTRUCTION BY ONE OF THE EPHRATA BRETHREN.

SPECIMENS OF GERMAN HANDICRAFT, XVIII CENTURY.
STIEGEL GLASSWARE, MADE IN LANCASTER COUNTY.

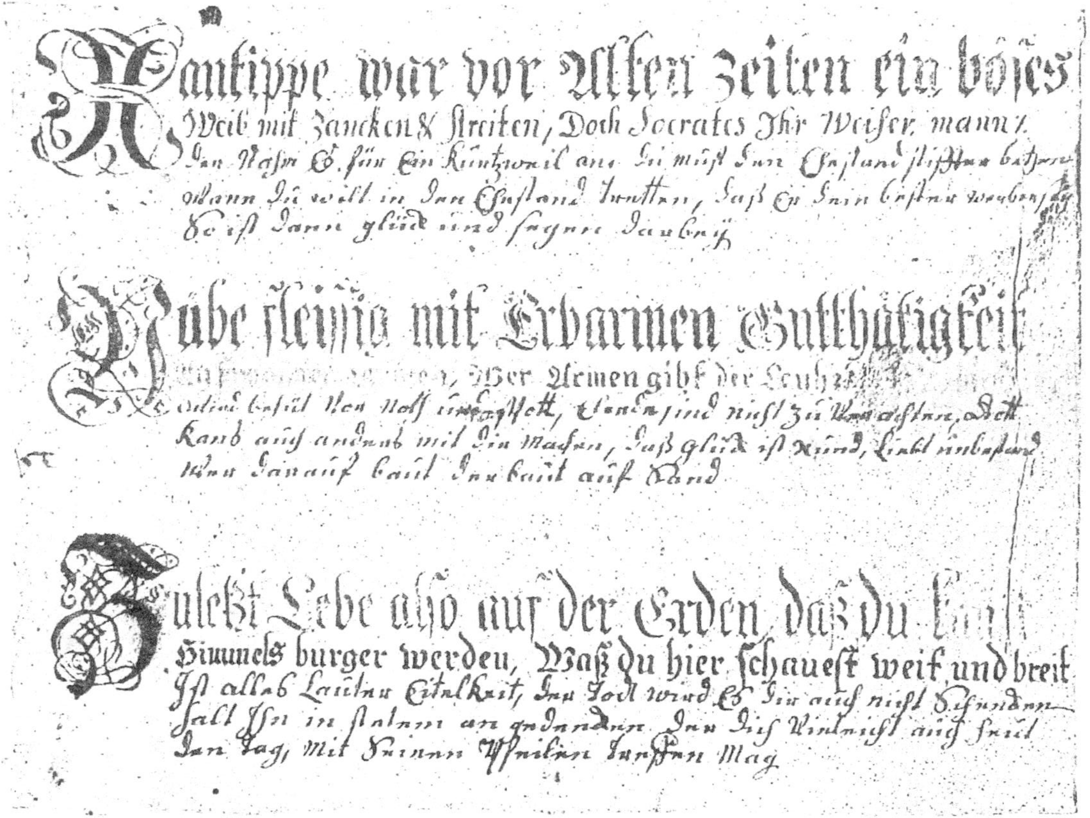
Xantippe war vor Alten zeiten ein böses
Weib mit Zancken & streiten, Doch Socrates Ihr Weiser mann
Übe fleissig mit Erbarmen Gutthätigkeit
Wer Armen gibt der
Zuletzt Lebe also auf der Erden daß du kanst
Himmels burger werden, Waß du hier schauest weit und breit

SPECIMEN OF EARLY GERMAN PENMANSHIP, BY CHRISTOPHER DOCK,
THE GERMAN SCHOOLMASTER ON THE SKIPPACH.

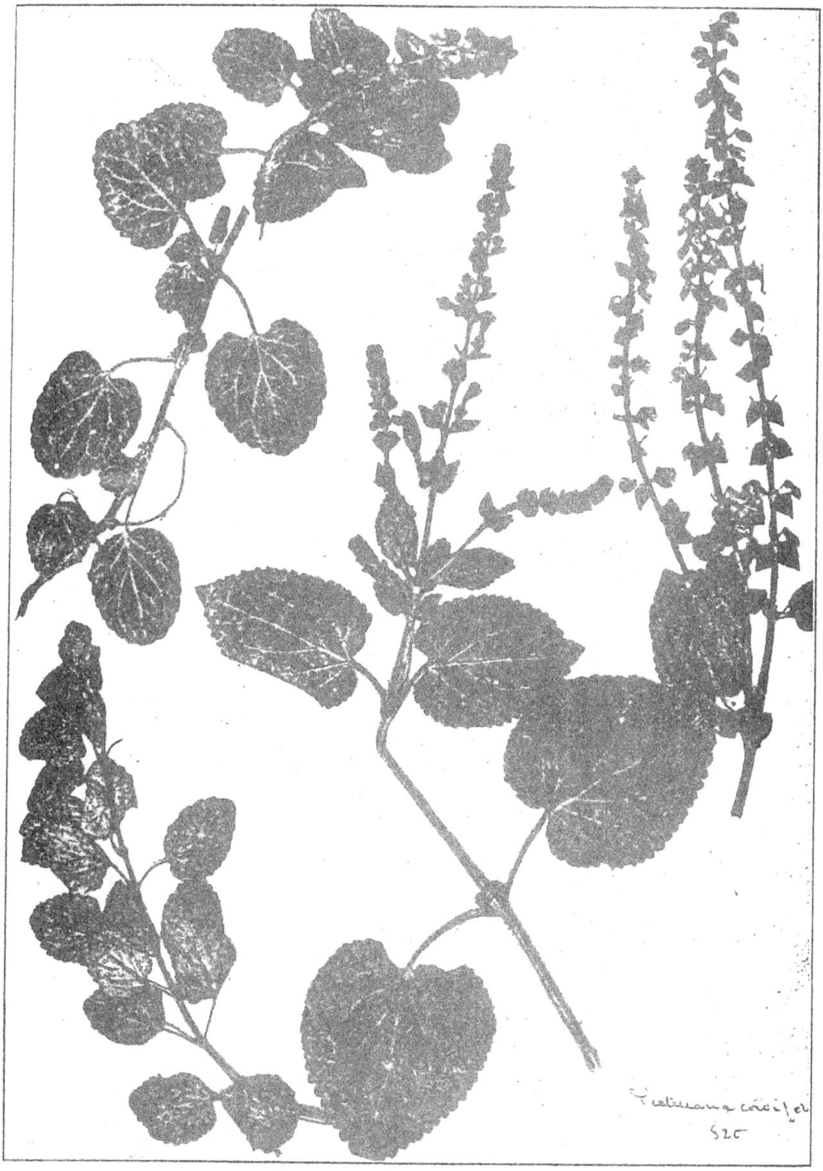

A PAGE FROM MUHLENBERG'S HERBARIUM.

"SCUTELLARIA CORDIFOLIA."

PHOTO. BY J. F. SACHSE.

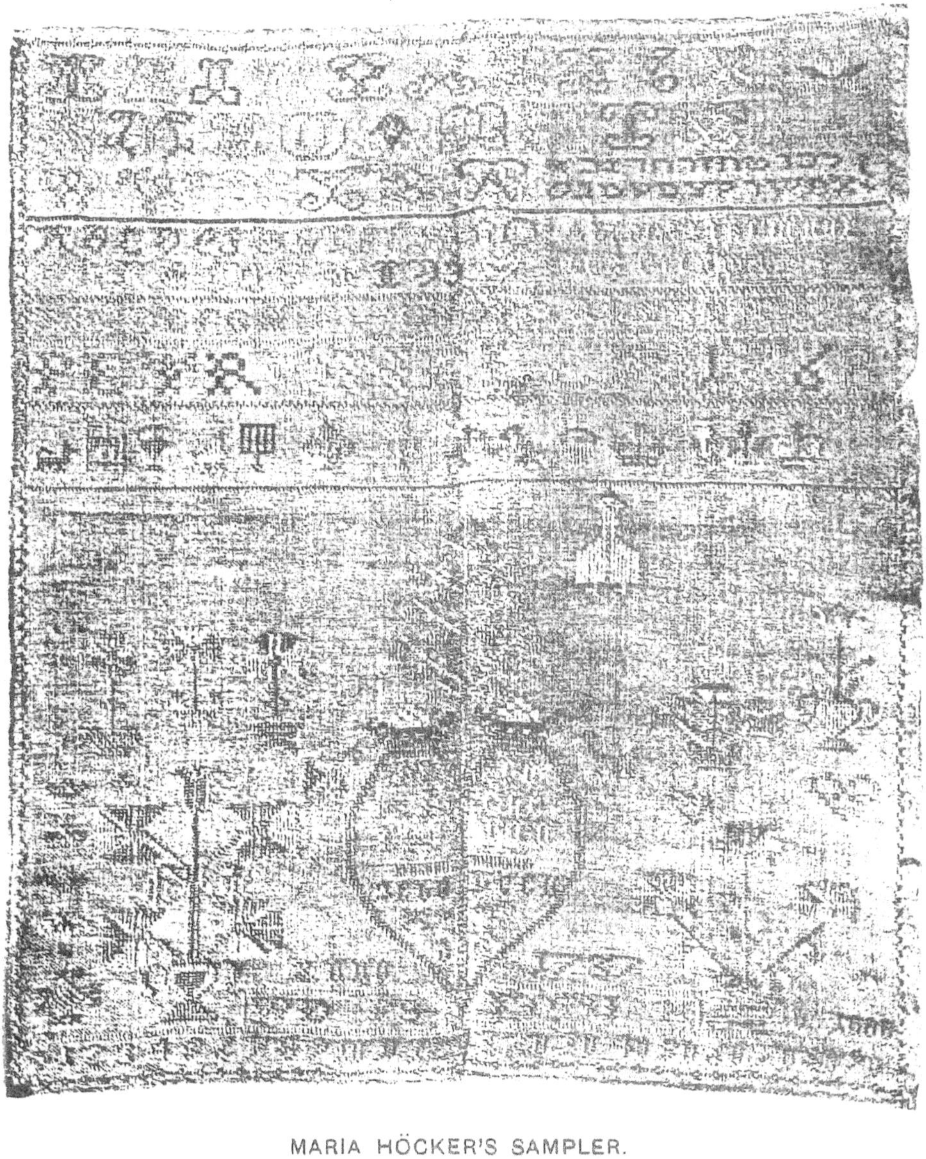

MARIA HÖCKER'S SAMPLER.

A SPECIMEN OF WOMAN'S HANDICRAFT, EPHRATA, 1765.

ONE OF THE EPHRATA PRINTING PRESSES, WHICH PRESSES SENT FORTH SO MANY WORKS OF TYPOGRAPHICAL ART INTO PROVINCIAL PENNSYLVANIA.

IN POSSESSION OF THE HISTORICAL SOCIETY OF PENNSYLVANIA.

2. German Pioneer Life and Domestic Customs

By

F.J.P. Schantz

This section is a facsimile of material which appeared originally as: F.J.P. Schantz, *The Domestic Life and Characteristics of the Pennsylvania-German Pioneer: A Narrative and Critical History Prepared at the Request of the Pennsylvania-German Society*, (Lancaster, Pa.: Pennsylvania-German Society, 1900.

CONTENTS.

CHAPTER V.

CHAPTER VI.

CHAPTER VII.

CHAPTER VIII.

CHAPTER IX.

CHAPTER X.

CHAPTER XI.

CHAPTER XII.

APPENDIX.

LIST OF PLATES.

ILLUSTRATIONS.

PREFATORY.

THERE is only one Pennsylvania in the world. Its citizens have many reasons to be proud of the relation which it sustains to the great union of States. Before the beginning of Pennsylvania and its gradual expansion to its present limits, the territory which it embraces existed for thousands of years and though the hunting ground of Indians for a long time, it was before the settlements by white men, simply a wonderful expansion of territory, rich in natural resources, to become the dwelling place of a great population. Its rivers and lesser streams followed their respective courses, the great valleys with their rich soil were long waiting to be turned into fields and meadows. The extensive forests on lowlands, on ridges and on mountain side, rich in timber, constituted a vast supply, to be of use to those, whom God might in due time lead to settle here. The earth itself covered valuable deposits, which should in due time be of great service to men. The rich deposits of limestone, iron, zinc, slate, coal, coal oil and cement-making stone and other materials were all here. Truly a wonderful country with vast resources. Before white men came here the wigwam of the Indian and his trail along streams and through forests were the only impress of human beings on this vast territory. The rivers and lesser streams were full of fish, wild animals and birds of many names were abundant, uncultivated trees and vines yielded their fruit in season. How strangely white men must have been affected, when they first viewed this vast expanse of country—its rivers with no sign of human life, but the red man in his canoe, its solid ground without roads and the habitations of civilized human beings.

And yet this was the country to be named Pennsylvania and to be filled in the course of time by a population that now numbers millions, to be met in great cities, in inland towns, in rural districts, in farming regions, in mines and in industries of every variety, with happy homes, with schools and churches, with public buildings, with business houses, with improved methods of travel, of business exchanges and of communication of thoughts to others.

White men came to Pennsylvania; Swedes settled on the Delaware as early as 1638, Hollanders located in the Minnisink region along the Delaware, north of the Blue Mountains at an early period, the settlements on the Delaware at and near Philadelphia in 1682, were followed by the arrival of Penn and German colonists. Immigrants came from different countries and occupied parts of the new colony. Germans who had first located along the Hudson, the Mohawk and the Schoharie, made the memorable journeys and settled on the Tulpehocken, the Swatara and the Quitapahilla. Thousands of immigrants came by the way of the port of Philadelphia and increased the number of settlers.

Whilst due credit is to be given to the English, the Welsh, the Scotch-Irish, the Hollander, and those of other nationalities for their part in the making of Pennsylvania, the German and Swiss immigrants are of special interest to us. We have been favored with full presentations of the life of the immigrant in the Fatherland, the journey down the Rhine and to England, the varied experiences of the long ocean journey, when months were required to reach the new world, the heroic move of Palatinates from the Schoharie to the Tulpehocken, and the arrival of the thousands of German immigrants through the port of Philadelphia and the varied conditions in which they reached this western shore.

They came to settle in the new world and in the consideration of their history in this country it is in order to present the first want of the settlers and how it was met. They came not like an army to be encamped for a season in one part of the country and then to remove to another and to be thus without a fixed habitation. Their first desire was to secure a home in this new country.

We turn then with pleasure to the consideration of the topic as announced:

The Domestic Life and Characteristics of the Pennsylvania-German Pioneer.

The German immigrant came from the fatherland in which the institution of marriage was held to be of divine appointment. The Catechism in the plain form in which it is to be taught by the head of the family, contains in the decalogue the divine commandment, "Honor thy Father and thy Mother," and presents the duties of children towards parents and superiors. The early records of congregations in this western world contain with the entries of other ministerial acts, the careful entries of marriages and of the baptism of children. Whilst some of those who settled in the new world formed communities with separate quarters for brethren and sisters—the great body of German immigrants settled as families.

The immigrants who came with larger means fared differently than those who came with limited funds. The man of means could soon secure a large tract of land and was able to erect a comfortable house. But the greater number of immigrants had but limited means and many were very poor and had become redemptioners.

CHAPTER I.

The Founding of a Home.

A HOUSE to dwell in and other buildings to meet existing necessities were the first wants of the German immigrant. Whilst the man of means could erect a comfortable dwelling, those of limited means and poverty were very glad when a log house could be erected. Before the erection of the log dwelling some men dwelt in caves along the river's bank, others under the wide spreading branches of great trees, in hastily constructed huts or under tents. The first log house was of very plain construction. The abundance of timber afforded material for its erection. Its sides were of logs, the openings between logs were filled with clay often mixed with grass. Windows were of small dimensions. Doors were often of two parts, an upper and a lower, hung or fastened separately. The interior was frequently only one room, with hearth and chimney, with the floor of stone or hardened clay, with steps or a ladder leading to the attic, with roughly constructed tables and benches, plainly made bedsteads, shelving on the walls and wooden pegs driven into logs. In this plain structure the pioneer deposited the limited means brought from the fatherland or secured here upon his arrival. In such a building the pioneer and his family had their first home in the new world.

Not all log houses were of such limited dimensions, many were larger and with wooden floors, with the space within the four sides divided into rooms on the first floor and in the attic. The pioneer and his descendants had as their dwellings in successive periods of time, first the log house of plainest construction, secondly, the new log structure of enlarged dimensions, with a good cellar, with logs for sides of building carefully prepared and well joined, with windows and doors of better make, with the interior division of a wide central hall and with rooms varying in number on the first floor, the attic also properly divided into rooms, and when a second story was added before the addition of the attic the inclosed space furnished additional rooms. The first log house often served only until a stone structure could be erected. In some localities houses were built of imported bricks. At a very early day bricks were made in this country. The abundance of stones furnished materials for the erection of substantial houses. These substantial stone buildings varied in size and style, often they were good solid structures of limited dimensions, but frequently they were larger buildings of two stories, with a large attic. The pioneer's house was not complete without the large hearth and chimney often in the center of the building and very often on one of the sides of the house with hearth and chimney erected outside of the building yet joining the same. Many of the buildings erected by the pioneers and their descendants were arranged to serve as forts in case of attacks by Indians, hence the very small, narrow windows in some of the buildings and the attic built in such manner as to extend considerably over the four sides of the building to allow openings from which the occupants of the house could repel attacks upon the building. The pioneer's house was seldom without a porch, at first of limited dimensions, but later of equal length with that of the house itself. Besides the dwelling house, other buildings were erected.

The barn and other structures for the shelter of live stock and the storing of the products of the field, the meadow and the orchard were erected as rapidly as the means of the pioneer increased. The spring house, the wood house and the large bake oven and smoke house under one roof were also added in good time.

It was not difficult to make an inventory of the contents of the dwelling house. The large hall had but little furniture besides a long, wooden chest, and a few benches or chairs. The best room of the house on one side of the hall contained a table, benches and later chairs, a desk with drawers, and the utensils used on the special hearth in heating the room. In the rear of the best room was the Kammer (bedroom) with its bed of plain make, also the trundel bed for younger children and the cradle for the youngest, a bench or a few chairs and the chest of drawers. The room on the other side of the hall was often not divided, but when divided the front room was called the living room (die Wohnstube) with table and benches or plain chairs, with closet for queensware and the storage of precious parcels, with the spinning wheel, with a clock as soon as the family could possess one, and with shelving for the books brought from the fatherland or secured in this country.

The kitchen contained the large hearth, often very large, with rods fastened to a beam and later an iron bar, from which descended chains to hold large kettles and pots used in the preparation of food; the tripod also on the hearth to hold kettles and pans used daily by the faithful housewife; the large dining table with benches on two long sides and short benches or chairs at each end; the large table for the use of those who prepared meals for the family; extensive shelving for holding tin and other ware; benches for water buckets and other vessels and the long and deep mantel shelf above the hearth on which many articles were placed. The second story of the house contained bed rooms and often a storage room. The bed rooms were furnished with beds, tables, large chests, and wooden pegs on the partitions. The attic was of great service for the storage of articles of the mechanism of man, and the preservation of fruits of the field, the garden, the orchard and the forest.

The cellar was an important part of the dwelling, with its provision for keeping food prepared from day to day and for the storage of abundant supplies gathered and kept in bins, tubs and barrels.

CHAPTER II.

Domestic Economy.

Wappen von Marienwerder.

THE pioneer's first want was a dwelling and the second was food for himself and family. The first year was often one of many privations, and one in which the closest economy was necessary. The earliest settlers used provisions brought from foreign lands. By means of these and such as they found in this country their wants were supplied until they were able to secure from fields, gardens and forests their daily bread. Wild animals of the forest, fowls of various names and fish that abounded in rivers and smaller streams were a rich provision for the pioneer before domestic animals supplied animal food. The first great want was that of grain and vegetables. The first flour had often to be carried great distances. After the first clearing of land, preparation of soil, sowing of seed and harvest of crops, the pioneer experienced many hardships in carrying grain to the distant mill and returning to his home with the supply of flour secured for himself and family. The first gathering of the garden's yield was likewise of great benefit and importance. After the first years of hardship had passed, the pioneer family had an abundance of food. As fields were enlarged they yielded increased harvests, and gardens and parts of fields supplied vegetables. In the course of time fruit trees and vines added their contributions and domestic animals and fowls in great numbers made animal food abundant.

Indian girl grinding corn.

Some supplies brought from foreign lands could at first be secured only at places far distant from the settler's home. In later years—new centers of supplies were opened in towns and villages in different localities. The proper supply of food was a great blessing for the pioneer and family.

The preparation of food in those early years was an important work of the mother and daughters of the household. At first they had only the hearth and bake oven; later they were favored with stoves built of suitable material. Many years passed before stoves made of iron could be bought. The modern cook stove and ranges of wonderful construction brought a great change.

The early settler knew nothing of coal, coal oil and burning gas. His burning material was wood. He had no matches to ignite the same. The tinder box with flint, steel and punk was of great service. The sun glass could be used only on days when the sun shone brightly. The flashing of powder in the pan of a gun was often necessary to secure fire. No wonder that at night, the burning log was carefully covered with ashes, that on the coming morning embers might be found to secure fire for the new day.

The pioneer had no hydrant, no turbine wheels and pipes, no tanks on the attic to supply the kitchen with water. It had to be carried from the spring — or first drawn from the well and then brought to the house—before pumps were secured. In the early days of settlers, men knew nothing of the modern refrigerator and dumb waiter. The cellar under the house and later the ground cellar with many steps leading down to the arch of necessary dimensions, the spring house, the smoke house and the attic of the dwelling house had to be reached to secure the supplies for the three meals of each day.

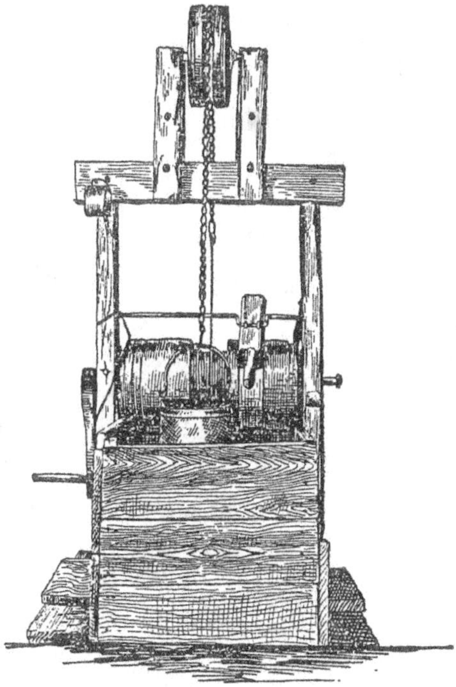

Primitive well curb, windlass and pulley.

The good housewife had her trials in the preparation of food. The tripod on the hearth held kettles and pans and other vessels; the iron rod or chain fastened to the bar in the chimney held kettles over the burning wood on the floor of the hearth. The bake oven served not only for baking bread but also in the preparation of other food. The large iron pot placed over the fire had a special cover, with a heavy rim, to hold burning coal on the cover, and was thus of varied service. The preparation of food was no easy work—it had to be attended to regularly and with great care. A failure on baking-days affected the whole family. A lack of supplies for a single meal could not be met or amended by a hasty visit of the baker, the butcher or the grocer.

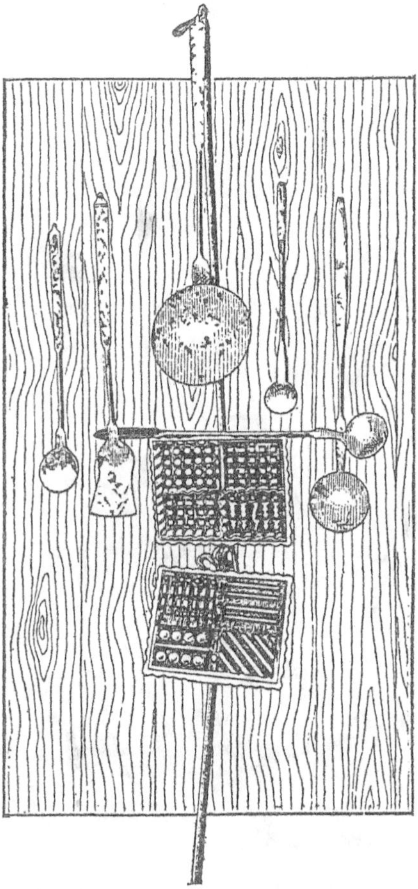

Küchen geschirr (kitchen utensils) —waffle iron, skimmers, ladles and pancake turner.

The table of the pioneer and his descendants was for many years of plain but substantial make. Before and long after a full supply of chairs could be secured benches afforded seats at the table. Table cloths were not always used. The first dishes were pewter and later of domestic earthenware and pottery. Platters, plates, bowls and other vessels held the prepared food. Individual plates, cups and saucers, and knives and forks were not wanting. Food was often conveyed from a large dish directly to the mouth of the eater. When such was the custom, each person was required to keep to his own place in the platter. The ordinary meal was plainly served. On special occasions the table bore abundant evidence of special preparation. Napkins and finger bowls were not always used. The basin and towel near the water bucket, well or spring were for such service.

With many preparations of cereals boiled or baked; with soups of meat broth, milk, eggs, cereals, vegetables and spices; with animal food smoked, roasted, broiled, fried or boiled; with vegetables of numerous names; with fruit stewed,. preserved or boiled like applebutter; with bread, butter, cheese of various makes; with pies of plain dough or raised dough and various contents; with puddings of many names; with cakes baked in the oven, prepared in the pan or in heated lard; with water, milk, coffee made of boiled, dried and roasted barley, rye or wheat, for ordinary use and genuine coffee on special occasions; tea made of herbs for common use, and imported tea for visitors and the household, when such were together at the table; the early settlers and their descendants had good, substantial, wholesome food; they fared well and did not suffer from dyspepsia and other stomachical troubles.

The housewife and daughter of the first century had no opportunity to attend special cooking schools, nor had they the use of large cook books, now so common. Mothers taught their daughters to prepare food and it was considered no disgrace for a daughter to serve with a family that needed help, where she could learn more of good housekeeping, including cooking. The Pennsylvania-German housewife has had through all the years dating from the settlement of this State the reputation of being a superior cook, and may her posterity never lose it! There seems at present no danger that she will change in this respect, for no one is more ready to make use of books and journals to condemn what is faulty and to approve what is to be commended, in the light of what she has been taught by her mother and grandmother.

Some people are disposed to become merry at the mention of the following: "Grumbire Supp und Mehl Supp," "Sauer Kraut und Speck," "Schnitz und Knöpf," "Gefüllter Säumage und Zitterle," "Brotwürscht und Lewerwürscht," "Wälschhahne und Gänz," "Ente und Hinkel," "Rindsflesch und Kalbflesch," "Aepfelküchelcher und Drechter Kuche," "Fett Kuche und Fastnacht Kuche," "Schnitz-boi und Zucker Kuche," "Leb Kuche und Weck," "Essig-Punsch und Heemgemacht Beer" and "Zuckersach und Nüsse"[1]—and yet these names would have appeared in the menu of the ancestors if such had been printed in their day.

[1] "Potato Soup and Meal Soup," "Sour Kraut and Fat Pork," "Dried Apples and Dough Buttons," "Filled Pig Stomach and Souse," "Sausage and Liver Pudding," "Turkey and Goose," "Duck and Chicken," "Beef and Veal," "Apple Fritters and Funnel Cakes," "Fat Cakes and Shrove Tide Cakes," "Dried-apple Pies and Sugar Cakes," "Gingerbread and Rusks," and "Vinegar Punch and Home-made Beer."

Vignette from an old schoolbook.

CHAPTER III.

Cultivating the Soil.

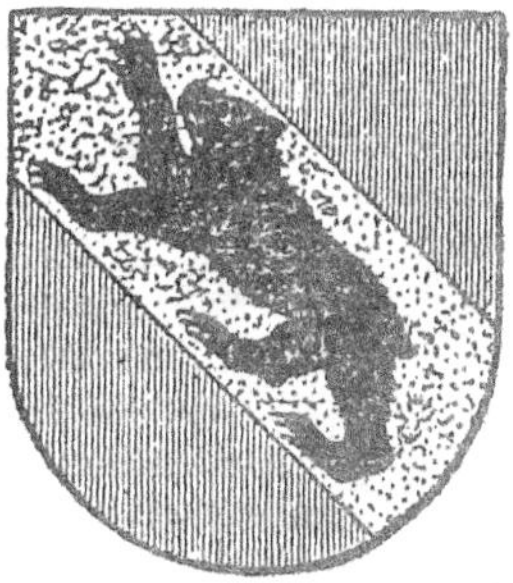

Wappen von Bern.

IT was a stupendous work that the pioneer had to perform. The log house was built where all of mother earth was in its primitive condition. Gardens, orchards, grain-yielding fields, and extensive fields and clean meadows with only grass covering the same were wanting. Where the earth was without scrub oak and great forest trees, weeds, briars and stones were in abundance. Even the making of a garden required days of arduous labor in the removal of weeds, briars and stones and in picking, digging and raking the ground before the deposit of seeds. The first harvest could only be expected after the preparation of a tract of land. This work embraced the removal of all that would prevent the raising of a crop, hence the removal of lighter growths by use of the axe, the saw, the pick and fire. The felling of trees, the removal of timber or its destruction by fire and the removal of stones were no light work. In the preparation of the ground the poorer settler had often only the use of pick, shovel and rake. Those who were fortunate enough to have a plough and harrow of the most primitive make, drawn by cattle, when horses were still wanting, were considered to be better prepared for the necessary work. The preparation of the ground was followed by the sowing of seed by hand. The enclosure of ground under cultivation required wearisome labor. The felling of trees, the cutting and sawing of the same in proper lengths, the splitting into rails, required much time and hard labor. The removal of all incumbrances from land and the opening of water courses for irrigation to secure good meadows were also necessary. Whilst waiting for the growth of the seed sown and the ripening of the harvest, the pioneer was busy in extending the borders of land to be cultivated. Hence the further felling of trees and the removal of wood to be used for a variety of purposes, as well as the transfer of wood to be burned on the hearth, added to the pioneer's work.

When the time for cutting grass and gathering the harvest arrived, all of the household were busy from early dawn to the close of day. The dengel stock, the hammer and the whetstone were of service in the preparation of the scythe and sickle. Grass was mowed by the use of the former. The wooden fork was used in turning the mowed grass, and the hand rake in gathering the hay on heaps before its removal to the primitive barn or stable, or the formation of stacks in the open air.

Grain was cut by the use of the sickle before the cradle came into use. Rakers and binders followed to make sheaves and shocks. The removal of the gathered harvest to barn or stables, or to places where it was stacked, followed in due time.

During hay-making and harvesting the laborers had, besides breakfast, dinner and supper, luncheon in the morning and in the afternoon, served under a tree by the good mother and her aids. An abundance of cold meats, bread, butter, cheese, applebutter, pickles, radishes, cakes, pies and varied beverages were freely served.

The gathering of corn and other products of the field followed later in each year and kept the husbandman busy. New attention had to be given to the soil for new sowing of seed and the expectation of a harvest in another year and required the new use of the plough and harrow.

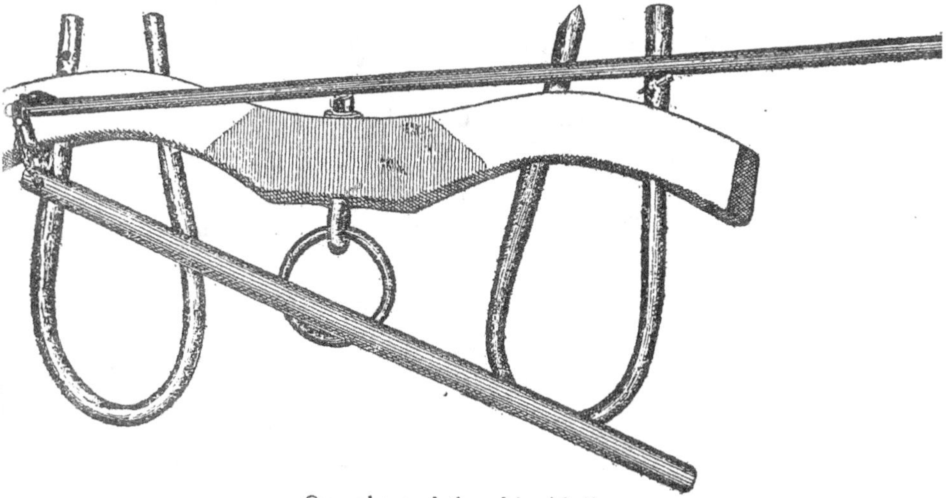

Ox yoke and threshing flail.

When fall arrived and winter came men were busy in separating grain from straw and ear. The use of the flail was common. Animals were used in treading out grain. The separation of grain from refuse was trying work, but it was necessary to secure grain for food.

But this work did not end the labors of the pioneer. In order to have grain turned into flour and other forms for man and beasts, it was necessary to take grain to the mill, which was often at a great distance from the home of the husbandman. Those who had no beast of burden were obliged to carry grain on their backs to the mill and return home with the flour they had secured. Such as had horses or oxen made use of the same in carrying grain to the mill and bringing home flour and other products. Later when wagons, often with a very primitive kind of wheels, made of sections of sawed logs, were secured, the ox team was of great service in carrying grain to the mill. Winter did not allow the pioneer to be idle. The daily duties at home, the preparation of wood for the hearth, the care of domestic animals, the hunting of wild animals for food and valuable skins, kept him busy. New attacks had to be made on the trees of the forest, that new soil might be made ready for enlarged harvests. When spring came the ground had to be put in order for spring sowing and planting.

In the course of years when orchards yielded their abundant crops new labors were necessary. When the yield of the fields, the orchard, the meadow and forest became more than what was necessary for the pioneer's home wants, he had supplies to take to the distant market. The long journey to the markets gave those who visited the same the most varied experiences. In the earliest years Philadelphia was the nearest market. So for the pioneer's son, who for the first time accompanied his father to the city, the trip afforded an opportunity to see many things that were entirely new to him.

Those who see Pennsylvania today in its advanced state of cultivation and observe what has been accomplished by the introduction of agricultural and other implements used in the cultivation of the soil, the sowing of seed, the reaping of the harvest, must ever remember the arduous work of the pioneer and his descendants, who, before the introduction of modern implements, brought a great portion of Pennsylvania under productive cultivation.

Whilst every pioneer needed a home and food and all were engaged in labor, not all were exclusively husbandmen. Nearly every home had its garden and tract of land to be cultivated. Even in towns and villages residents had gardens and often orchards near their dwellings and frequently lots at no great distance, which were carefully cultivated. The miller, the sawmiller, the carpenter, the cabinet-maker, the blacksmith, the tinsmith, the potter, the weaver, the fuller, the tanner, the tailor, the shoemaker, the clock-maker, the gunsmith, the paper-maker, the printer, the bookbinder, the merchant, the distiller, the innkeeper, the officers of the colony, the lawyer, the doctor of medicine and the minister of the Gospel were all engaged in work. There was an abundance of work and no necessity for the life of the tramp, who would eat and yet not toil.

The pioneer was a true expansionist. Where once only the log house and the simple structure for the protection of animals and the storing of field and meadow products and the enclosed small garden, and the limited number of acres under cultivation were to be seen, there appeared in the course of years, the large, well-built dwelling house, the immense barn and many other buildings for various uses, the large garden, the beautiful shade and fruit trees and vines near the dwelling, the extensive orchard, the beautiful meadows, the many large fields bearing a variety of crops, the carefully made roads and lanes and the long lines of fences enclosing the different parts of the farm. Whilst the dwelling sheltered the family, the buildings of the farmyard sheltered horses, cattle, sheep, swine and many of the feathered tribes. The products of the farm were so abundant that no one had occasion to suffer hunger, and the supplies for the market became so great that other means of transportation than the farm wagon were hailed with joy by those who appreciated the advantages extended by the same.

Harvest scene, from an old reader.

CHAPTER IV.

Wearing Apparel of the German Settlers.

Wappen von Uri.

WE now come to the consideration of the wearing apparel of the pioneer. The immigrants wore at first garments brought from the fatherland. The quantity brought depended on the ability to procure the same. The immigrants were often deprived of their supply of clothing by the heartless sea captains and their associates who, in view of exorbitant extra charges during the sea voyage, compelled the immigrant, who had not sufficient money to pay, to surrender garments to meet their demands. To replenish the supply—whilst no doubt those, who were able to do so, secured imported goods for new garments—the great body of settlers found it necessary to meet this want by raising flax and later by raising sheep for furnishing a supply of wool, so that materials for clothing and other uses could be secured in this new world.

From the sowing of the flax seed to the completion of the tow or linen garment there was work for men and women. Men prepared the soil and selected the best part of a field for sowing flax seed. It was sown at the time oats were

"Woll-rad" or "Zwirn-rad," "Wheel for Spinning Wool" or "Twisting-Wheel."

sown—and usually in the same field. It was gathered a few weeks before oats harvest. It was drawn with the roots in bunches, which were tied separately and shocked. Ten to twelve bunches formed a shock. It was allowed to stand on the field until the tops became dry and brown. Straw-binders were laid on the ground, the flax placed on the same, and larger bundles formed, which were taken to the barn floor. Here the seed end of the flax was beaten on an elevated plank or on a barrel, to remove the seed, which was separated from the chaff by means of a fan (worfschaufel) and at a later period by a wind mill. The flax seed was carefully stored, as it was a valuable product to supply an oil which commanded a high price. The flax was rebound and taken to a clean part of the field, where it was spread on the ground and allowed to remain a few weeks until rain and sunshine had made the inner part of the flax brittle and the outer part tough. It was rebound and removed to the barn or other building where it could be kept. Then followed the breaking of the flax. The first requirement was a fireplace and a fire, over which, on elevated bars or rails, the flax was laid and dried to become more brittle. The flax breakers, often four or five in number, surrounded the fireplace and broke the flax as best they could and in time on a flax break. When this process was ended, the flax was rebound in bundles containing twenty-five handfuls and again taken to the barn. Then followed the first hackling to separate the boll of the flax. This was done on a coarse hackle. The flax was then swingled on a board or plank by means of a wand or wooden knife, and in later years on a break wheel. After the swingling followed hackling on a hackle screwed to the top of a bench. The hackle consisted of a board about ten inches long and three or four

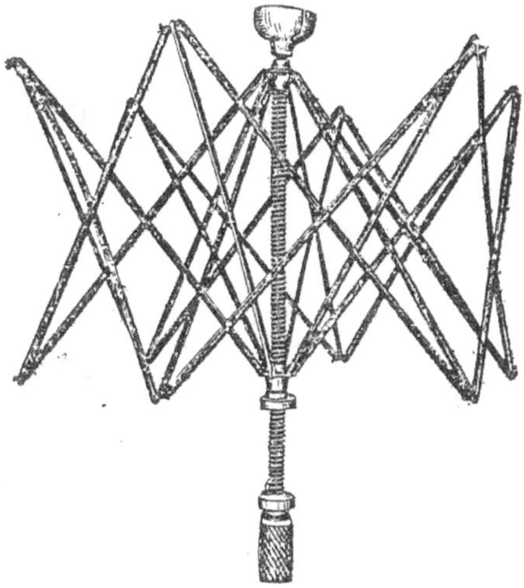

Faden-haspel (Thread reel) on which strands were stretched and then wound into a ball.

inches wide, into which wrought-iron nails about five inches long had been driven. The hackling separated the tow from the fine flax and thus yielded tow and flax. The tow was placed in boxes or barrels and the flax was formed into switches, the ends of which were joined, and a number of such switches were united by a cord and kept in bundles.

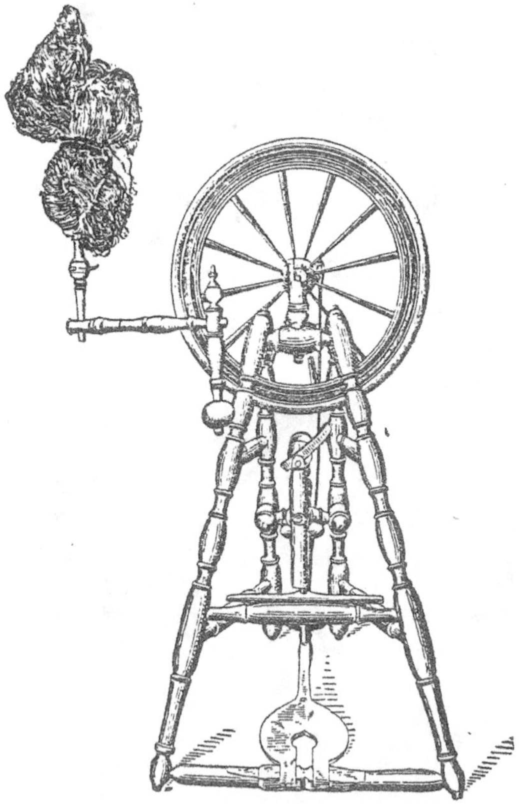

Upright spinning wheel.

The spinning of tow and flax, the work of mothers and daughters, who rose early and often retired late, required much time and labor. The spinning wheel and reel were not wanting. The spinning of tow was first in order.

The tow was placed on the fork of the wheel and spun. The spinning of flax, which was wound on a specially made holder, was done on the same wheel on which tow was spun. The reel (haspel) was used for winding the spun tow and flax. One hundred and forty-four revolutions of the reel marked by the indicator were required for a cut. These were formed into skeins, a skein of tow containing four cuts and one of flax six cuts. The skeins of spun tow and flax were boiled in a mixture of ash and water—to make the same soft and tender, and were subsequently laid on grass or hung on bars to dry and to be bleached.

In weaving the same loom was used for making tow cloth and linen with different gearing for each. The woven material was usually one yard wide. After the web had been made ready a part of it was glued (geschlicht). Whilst time was given for drying the weaver was busy in spooling, and thus there was a constant change from weaving to spooling. Tow cloth was often of different stripes. The woof for the same was colored yellow by means of the bark of hickory trees or peach leaves and blue with indigo. After weaving, plain tow cloth and linen were washed, spread on grass, sprinkled regularly and given time to bleach. The proper bleaching often required several weeks of time. The materials thus obtained and linen thread of various thicknesses, also spun at home, were now ready for use.

The tow cloth was used for clothing, bedding, table cloths, towels, bags, coverings and other articles. Linen cloth of various degrees of fineness was used for shirts, summer clothing, bedding, table cloths, towels and many other purposes.

Linen goods were often checked goods—made of linen colored differently.

In the course of years the pioneer and his descendants raised sheep. A husbandman would have from ten to twelve—but frequently also from twenty to twenty-five or more sheep. Sheep shearing was in order in May of each year. The wool secured was washed and then dried on grass. It was then carefully cleaned and picked so that no impurities might remain. It was taken to the carding mill, where it was first carded on rollers, on which there were strips of leather filled with fine wires and fine nails and then passed between rollers on which there were ribs which formed the rolls of wool, which dropped from the cylinders. The wool, after being thus formed into rolls, was taken home, where it was spun on the large and small spinning wheels. The weaving of wool was the same as that of tow and flax. When the supply of wool was yet limited, in weaving the webb was often the product of flax and the woof of wool. The material obtained was known as the linsey-woolsey. It was a much better material for winter clothing than tow cloth and linen cloth, and extensively used for such purposes. Cloth woven entirely of wool was for best clothing for wear on Sunday and special occasions. The woolen cloth was taken to the fulling-mill (walk mühle). Here it was placed in large receptacles, in which soap and water were used. The material was beaten and turned and when it was removed from the receptacles to be washed it was found narrower and thicker than before. It was then colored black, brown, gray, deep yellow or red. After being dried, trimmed and rolled it was ready to be taken to the owner's home and was ready for use. Flannels were of different colors and were used for dresses and undergarments.

In those primitive years and in many years that followed garments were made at home without any directions given by fashion books and without the aid of sewing machines. In later years tailors were engaged to come to the homes of families to make garments for men. The primitive mothers and daughters had an abundance of work in making garments for members of the household. They were also frequently engaged in knitting to supply the family with stockings, socks, mittens, scarfs and caps. They likewise spent much time in making from tow, linen and woolen materials a variety of articles for use and ornament in the home.

Shoes were not constantly worn. In summer many persons wore no shoes. In winter they were worn by all. During the summer they were, however, worn on special occasions. Tradition informs us that shoes were carried by hand by church-goers until the vicinity of the church was reached, when they were put on and removed again soon after the worshippers had left the church building. Shoemakers traveled and did not only mend shoes, but often also remained with a family to make shoes for all its members.

Wedding gown worn by a grandmother and a granddaughter.

Hats and caps worn by men were made in this country at a very early period. An abundance of materials for making the same was found here. Mothers and daughters made hoods at home. A bonnet of large dimensions was a desirable acquisition, to be made only by purchase in towns.

With the increase of wealth and opportunities to secure wearing apparel from the country store, the ancestors were also able to purchase other materials for various uses. There was a marked difference between clothing made of domestic materials and clothing made of store goods. People in the country began to follow the customs of the people dwelling in towns, and in the course of years people in the country also had fine clothing for their appearance on special occasions.

In earlier periods there was no constant change of fashions as in our day. The good clothing worn by parents was handed down to their children, who were not ashamed to wear the same. Garments were worn for a much longer time than in our day. The writer knew two men, who lived within the last fifty years, the one, the senior in years, remarked that whilst he wore a coat two years, the younger man was not satisfied without two new coats in each year. When journeys were made great care was taken of extra apparel, if made on foot the knapsack was carefully packed, if made on horseback then saddle bags were of great service, when made later on in wagons and coaches the requisites for the journey were placed in wallets, in strong paper and leathern boxes of varied style and in trunks covered with skins of animals.

CHAPTER V.

The Barnyard and its Denizens.

Wappen von Marburg.

ANOTHER important branch of the domestic life of the pioneer was the raising and care of domestic animals and fowls. The horse, ass, horned cattle, sheep, swine, dogs and cats were regarded as necessary. The peacock, turkey, goose, duck, chicken and pigeons supplied numerous wants. Whilst the log houses and stone structures were the dwellings of families, the barns, stables, sheds, cotes, kennels, hen-houses and dove cotes served for the protection of animals and fowls. The Pennsylvania-German has ever been known for his careful provision for the care of his live stock.

The horse and ass were of great service in farm work, in ploughing and harrowing the soil to be seeded, in the removal of hay and grain to the barn and to places where the same were stacked, in the threshing of grain, in carrying grain to the mills, in hauling stones from the fields, in supplying the field with manure and lime, in hauling wood for home use and timber to be sawed, and in carrying farm products to market places. They were also of service in the visitation of families, in the transaction of business at distant places, in attending church services and public gatherings and in extended journeys. No wonder that early settlers cared so well for their horses and were in favor of hanging horse thieves.

Horned cattle were also of great service. They often supplied the place of the horse and ass in farm work and in transportation. The cow supplied milk, from which cream, butter and cheese were obtained. The flesh of cattle furnished as a food, an abundance of veal and beef and of salted and smoked meats. Tallow served in making candles. The skins of animals, when tanned, furnished leather for shoes, harness and other purposes. Whole skins were of great service as covers. The excess of horned cattle not needed for domestic use formed a supply of the markets. The pioneer was engaged in stock raising, for pasture was abundant. Young stock was often driven in spring to distant places for pasturage and brought home in fall in good condition.

Swine served also for many purposes. Their raising in early days was not difficult. They were allowed to roam on commons and in forests in which they found an abundance of acorns and other nuts. The swine, when killed, supplied fresh pork, salt meats, sausages, hams and shoulders and also an abundance of lard for home use and the market. The lard lamp would have been of no use without a supply of lard. Butchering days were important days in the life of the pioneer.

Dogs and cats were prized by the pioneer. No picture of the early home would be complete without the dog and the cat. The dog was often the companion of his master in his work on the field and in the forest. He aided him in herding his cattle. He was his aid in capturing or driving off wild animals. He was the playmate of children in the home, but also the faithful guard of the homestead at night, promptly signaling the presence of the red man of the forest, and the approach of thieves and wild animals. No wonder that the faithfulness of the dog has often been the theme of writers.

The cat also rendered good service as the enemy of rats and mice and kept the house and other buildings as clear of these destructive creatures as it could. The cat's play often amused the inmates of the house. Its doleful cry at night often disturbed the slumbers of many. But no one would allow its banishment from the home.

Whilst the peacock, with its tail of long feathers of rich and elegant colors, was the pride of the barnyard, the turkey, goose, duck and chicken were raised not only for a supply of eggs, but also to be served on the table on special occasions. The feathers of some of them were used in filling pillow cases and ticks for the comfortable rest of the head and body of the weary and the cover of all sleepers in winter. The quill obtained from the goose afforded the pen for writing the love letter, the note of indebtedness, the receipt of money paid and the death warrant.

The surplus yield of feathers constituted one of the perquisites of the good housewife, and the money received for the same enabled her to purchase many articles of value, for personal use and gifts to others.

The mother of the household has always taken an interest in the raising of fowls, and the sale of the same furnished her money for many uses. The writer remembers that in the year 1867 he was collecting money for an important church work. He called at the houses of the different parishioners of a charge which he was visiting. At one of these homes the mother met him with a cheerful face and, as soon as he had stated the object of his call, said: "Yes, I have two dollars and a-half to give you," and added: "And I wish to tell you how it is that I have this money for you. I set a hen with turkey eggs and had a lot of fine little turkeys, which however a heavy rain killed for me. I felt very sorry. I said to the Lord that I would set another hen with turkey eggs, and that if turkeys would be hatched and I would be allowed to raise them and sell them I would give Him the one-tenth of the proceeds of the sale. The turkeys were hatched; I was successful in raising them, and sold them on the market for twenty-five dollars, and now I will keep the promise I made to the Lord." She handed the two dollars and a-half to the writer, and they are today a part of the endowment of a fine institution of learning.

The writer remembers that a daughter in a rural home had in the sixties of the closing century a novel method of awakening her guests, which she said she had learned from a professor of music, who had once stopped for a night at her home. He had severe toothache and could not sleep. He rose early in the morning and after a walk returned to the house, entered the parlor and played a number of selections on the piano. She was awakened by the music and so delightfully entertained, that she concluded in future to use this method of awakening her guests. She observed her rule when the writer was a guest at her home, and when he met the family in the morning, she told him the above and added: "I play first a grand march to awaken my guests, then a polka and a waltz to entertain them, and last of all a choral to signify that it is time to rise." But visitors in rural homes in earlier and later years have often been awakened by other sounds—the cry of the peacock, the gobbling of the turkey, the quacking of geese and ducks, the screeching of the guinea hen, the crowing of the rooster, the cackling of hens, the lowing of the cattle, the squealing of pigs and the barking of dogs.

While domestic animals yielded for the market a varied supply of meats, milk, butter, cheese, lard and tallow, and furnished hides for the tannery, the domestic fowls also furnished many supplies of eggs and coveted meats and yielded the settler a good reward for his toil in the care of animals and fowls.

Vignette from an old almanac.

CHAPTER VI.

Domestic Piety and Religion.

Wappen von Glogau.

THE German immigrants were generally Christian people. In the old fatherland they had enjoyed the privileges of churches and schools. They came to this western world with the faith which had been wrought in them by the Holy Ghost through the means of grace. Whilst but few came accompanied by pastors and teachers, they brought with them copies of the Bible, hymn-book, prayer-book, catechism, sermon-book and other devotional books. Court Chaplain Boehm, of London, rendered an important service to immigrants sent from England to America by securing for them copies of Arndt's *Wahres Christenthum*. Starke's *Gebet Buch* was also used by many settlers.

The pioneers, when settled in this country, longed for the favor of churches and ministers of schools and teachers

and others will in due time show how this want was supplied. But religion entered into the daily life of the settler, and on this account its consideration belongs to that of his domestic life.

Religious books brought by immigrants were often seized by sea captains on arrival in this country for the payment of most extravagant charges for services to immigrants during the sea voyage.

Religious books were imported from the fatherland and sold in this country and some were also donated. Copies of these and of such as were brought by the immigrants themselves are thus to be found among descendants of the pioneers and prized as heirlooms.

Des Geist- und Trostreichen Lehrers,
Herrn Johann Arndts,
Weyl. General-Superintendentens des Fürstenthums
Lüneburg,
Sämtliche Geistreiche Bücher
Vom Wahren
Christenthum,
handelnd von
heilsamer Buße / herzlicher Reu und Leid über die Sünde
und wahrem Glauben / auch heiligem Leben und Wandel
der rechten wahren Christen.
Nicht allein mit beygefügten Gebeten / Anmerckungen / Lebens-
lauf des Autoris, und nöthigen Registern;
Sondern auch
mit erbaulichen Sinnbildern und deren Erklärung,
und einer Catechetischen Einleitung von 188. Fragen
versehen.
Nebst dem
Paradies-Gärtlein,
in groben Druck
Und einigen besondern Registern / vermittelst welchen man
dieses Buch auf alle Sonn- und Festtages-Evangelia und Episteln
als ein ordentliches Haus-Postill-Buch wol gebrauchen kan,
vermehret.
Giessen / Verlegts Eberhard Heinrich [illegible]
[illegible]

German religious books were published in this country at a very early day. In 1708 Justus Falkner published the first book of a Lutheran minister printed in America, a treatise in questions and answers on the chief doctrines of the Christian religion. *The first century of German printing in America, 1728–1830*—by Oswald Seidensticker, Philadelphia, is an exceedingly interesting and valuable publication, from which the following facts, touching the publication of religious books in this country have been gathered.

In 1728 appeared *Das Büchlein vom Sabbath*, and *Neun und neunzig mystische Sprüche*, by Conrad Beissel, the former printed by Andrew Bradford, the latter by Benjamin Franklin.

Benjamin Franklin also printed for the religious enthusiasts of Lancaster County in 1730—*Götttiche Liebes und Lobesgethöne*, in 1732 *Vorspiel der Neuen Welt*, and in 1736 *Jacobs Kampf und Ritters-Platz*. In 1739 Christoph Sauer, of Germantown, printed *Zionitischer Weyrauchs Hügel oder Myrrhenberg* for the Ephrata Brethren. This was the first American book in German type. The book contains 654 hymns in 33 divisions, with an appendix of 38 hymns with separate title.[1]

ZIONITISCHER
Weyrauchs Hügel
Oder:
Myrrhen Berg,
Worinnen allerley liebliches und wohl riechendes nach Apotheker-Kunst zubereitetes Rauch-Werck zu finden.
Bestehend
In allerley Liebes-Würckungen der in GOTT geheiligten Seelen, welche sich in vielen und mancherley geistlichen und lieblichen Liedern aus gebildet.
Als darinnen
Der letzte Ruff zu dem Abendmahl des grossen GOttes auf unterschiedliche Weise trefflich aus gedrucket ist;
Zum Dienst
Der in dem Abend-Ländischen Welt-Theil als bey dem Untergang der Sonnen erweckten Kirche GOttes, und zu ihrer Ermunterung auf die Mitternächtige Zukunfft des Bräutigams ans Licht gegeben.
Germantown, Gedruckt bey Christoph Sauer.

In 1742, Christopher Sauer printed *Ausbund*, a large hymnbook highly esteemed by the Mennonites. In 1742, Sauer printed by order of Count Zinzendorf *Hirten-Lieder von Bethlehem*, a collection of 360 hymns.

In 1743 Christopher Sauer, of Germantown, printed *Biblia*, Das ist die Heilige Schrift Altes und Neues Testaments, nach der Deutschen Uebersetzung D. Martin Luthers, quarto, to which he added an appendix of his own: Kurtzer Begriff von der heil. Schrifft. This was the first bible printed in America in a European language. The type was obtained from Heinrich Ehrenfried Luther in Frankfurt, to whom Sauer made a present of twelve copies of

[1] For a full account of the issues of the Ephrata press, see German Sectarians of Pennsylvania, Volumes I. and II., by Julius F. Sachse, 1899.

his edition of the bible, all of which were given to distinguished persons.[1]

In 1744 he printed *Der Kleine Catechismus D. Martin Luthers. Mit Erläuterungen herausgegeben zum Ge-*

Der
kleine
Catechismus
D. Martin Luthers.
Mit Erläuterungen
herausgegeben
zum Gebrauch
der
Lutherischē Gemeinen
in
Pensylvanien.
Germanton
Gedruckt bey Christoph Saur.
1744.

brauch der lutherischen Gemeinen in Pennsylvanien. This catechism was edited, prefaced and annotated by Count Zinzendorf.

[1] For a critical account of Sauer and his German bible, see Sachse, German Sectarians, Volume II., pp. 1–68.

In 1744, there was issued by the same press *Das Kleine Davidische Psalterspiel der Kinder Zions.* This work became quite popular with some sects—Dunkers, Mennonites, etc.—as is evidenced by the numerous editions of the book. "Many of the hymns have the mystic coloring, sentimental style and bold allegorism found in the Ephrata books."

In 1745, Christopher Sauer printed *Das Neue Testament Unsers Herren und Heylandes Jesu Christi.* 12mo. This was the first separate edition of the New Testament printed by Sauer.[1]

In 1746, he published *Der Psalter des Königs und Propheten Davids.* Verteutscht von D. Martin Luthers. 16mo.

In 1747 appeared the first hymn-book printed at Ephrata entitled, *Das Gesäng der einsamen und Verlassenen Turtel-Taube, nemlich der Christlichen Kirche.* It contains only original material, consisting of 378 hymns, inclusive of those already in the Franklin books of 1730, 1732 and 1736.

In 1748 the Ephrata Brethren completed the printing of Tielman Jans van Braght's great work, translated into German from the Dutch and entitled in German *Der Blutige Schau-Platz oder Mätyrer-Spiegel der Tauffs-Gesinnten oder Wehrlosen Christen.* It appeared in two volumes, bound as one, the first containing Introduction 56 pages, Text 478 pages and the Index 6 pages, the second containing: Introduction 14 pages, Text 950 pages, and Index 8 pages. This splendid folio is the largest, and, in some respects, most remarkable book of the colonial period. Pennsylvania Mennonites requested their brethren in Holland in 1745 to have the book translated into

[1] Ibid.

Das Neue

Testament

Unsers

HErrn und Heylandes

JEsu CHristi,

Verteutscht

Von

D. Martin Luther.

Mit

Jedes Capitels kurtzen

Summarien,

Auch beygefügten vielen richtigen

Parallelen.

Germantown:

Gedruckt und zu finden bey Christoph Saur, 1745.

Title page of first edition of New Testament printed in America. See page 40.

German, but were not gratified. The Ephrata Brethren undertook the laborious task, making the translation, manufacturing the paper and doing the printing and binding.[1]

In 1749 Franklin and Böhm printed *Der Kleine Catechismus des sel. D. Martin Luther.*

In 1751 Benjamin Franklin and Johann Böhm printed *Arndt's Wahres Christenthum.* 8vo. Introduction, etc., 32 pages, the text 1,356 pages and 65 copper plate illustrations which were brought from Germany. This was the largest book printed in Philadelphia during the last century. The American preface was written by Rev. J. A. Christopher Hartwig, a Lutheran minister.

In 1752 Christopher Sauer published *Geistreiche Lieder*, a 12mo. hymn-book of 562 pages, containing beside the hymns, an index, catechism, prayers, gospels, epistles, and destruction of Jerusalem. This was the first Reformed hymn-book printed in America. In the same year he published *Der Kleine Catechismus des Seligen D. Martin Luther.* Nebst der Morgen- Tisch- und Abend-Gebeten—sieben Buss-Psalmen, ein Geistliches Lied und das Einmal Eins. In 1753 this was followed with *Die Kleine Geistliche Harfe*, a hymn-book for the use of the Mennonites. In 1753 he issued *Neu-vermehrt- und Vollständiges Gesang-Buch*, containing besides the hymns of *Geistreiche Lieder* published in 1752—the Psalms of David (L. Ambrosii translation) and the Heidelberg Catechism.

In 1753 the *Lancastersche Zeitung* contained an advertisement of Job. Habermann's Large Prayer Book. Both the large and a small edition of this prayer-book attained great popularity in America.

---

[1] Ibid., p. 222, et seq.

Der

Blutige Schau-Platz

oder

Martyrer

Spiegel der Tauffs Gesinnten

oder

Wehrlosen-Christen,

Die um des Zeugnuß JEsu ihres Seligmachers willen gelitten haben, und seynd getödtet worden, von Christi Zeit an bis auf das Jahr 1660.

Vormals aus unterschiedlichen glaubwürdigen Chronicken, Nachrichten und Zeugnüssen gesammlet und in Holländischer Sprach heraus gegeben

von T. J. V. BRAGHT.

Nun aber sorgfältigst ins Hochteutsche übersetzt und zum erstenmal ans Licht gebracht.

EPHRATA in Pensylvanien,

Drucks und Verlags der Brüderschafft. Anno MDCCXLVIII.

Title page of the celebrated Martyr Book. See page 40.

In 1754 the Ephrata Brethren printed on writing paper *Paradisisches Wunderspiel.*

In 1755 Christopher Sauer published a second edition of the New Testament in German.

In 1757 Benjamin Franklin and Anthony Armbruster published *Der Psalter Davids.*

In 1759 Christopher Sauer printed Habermann and Naumann's *Christliche Morgen- und Abend-Gebeten.*

In 1759 Christopher Sauer published *Vollständiges Marburger Gesang-Buch. Zur Beförderung des so Kirchen als Privat-Gottesdienstes. Mit erbaulichen Morgen-Abend-Buss-Beicht- und Communion-Gebetlein vermehret.* This was the first German Lutheran hymn-book published in America.

In 1761 Henrich Miller published Luther's Small Catechism translated into English by Rev. C. M. Wrangel, provost of the Swedish churches on the Delaware, and an intimate friend of Patriarch Muhlenberg.

In 1762 the Brotherhood of Ephrata published a new and enlarged edition of the hymn-book entitled *Die einsame Turtel Taube.* In the same year Christopher Sauer, Jr., published a hymn-book for the Schwenkfelders, containing 760 pages, a third edition of *Der Psalter des König und Propheten Davids* and a second edition of the *Marburger-Gesangbuch*, of which the first edition appeared in 1759.

In 1762 Anton Armbruster published *Kurtzgefaste Grund-Lehren des Reformirten Christenthums*, and Peter Miller & Co. published *Catechismus oder Kurzer Unterricht Christlicher Lehre* (in Reformirten Kirchen und Schuhlen).

In 1763 Christopher Sauer, Jr., published a second edition of the Germantown bible in German. In his preface

Paradisisches Wunder-Spiel,

Welches sich
In diesen letzten Zeiten und Tagen
In denen Abend-Ländischen Welt-Theilen als ein Vorspiel der neuen Welt hervor gethan. Bestehende
In einer gantz neuen und ungemeinen Sing-Art auf Weise der Englischen und himmlischen Chören eingerichtet.

Da dann das Lied Mosis und des Lamms, wie auch das hohe Lied Salomonis samt noch mehrern Zeugnüssen aus der Bibel und andern Heiligen in liebliche Melodyen gebracht. Wobey nicht weniger der Zuruf der Braut des Lamms, sammt der Zubereitung auf den herzlichen Hochzeit-Tag trefflich Praefigurirt wird.

Alles nach Englischen Chören Gesangs-Weise mit viel Mühe und grosem Fleiß ausgefertiget von einem

Friedsamen,

Der sonst in dieser Welt weder Namen noch Titul suchet.

EPHRATÆ Sumptibus Societatis: 1754.

he remarks: "So then the Holy Writ, called the Bible, appears on the American Continent for the second time in the German language to the renown of the German nation, no other nation being able to claim that the Bible has been printed in their language in this division of the globe."[1]

In the year 1763 the Germantown printer published *Der Kleine Darmstädtische Catechismus, Herrn D. Martin Luthers*, etc., also a second edition of the Reformed Hymn Book first published in 1753.

In 1763 Johann Brandmüller, of Friedensthal, near Bethlehem, published *The Harmony of the Gospels* and a hymn-book, both in the Delaware language. The translation was by Bernhard Adam Grube, a Moravian missionary.

In 1763 Henrich Miller printed *Catechismus oder Anfanlgicher Unterricht Christlicher Glaubens-Lehre*, a Schwenkfelder Catechism. He also printed in the same year "A hymn-book for the children belonging to the Brethren's (Moravian) Congregations."

In 1765 Christopher Sauer, Jr., published Johann Arndt's *Paradies-Gärtlein*.

In 1766 the most extensive collection of Ephrata hymns, numbering 725, entitled *Paradisisches Wunder-Spiel*, was published at Ephrata.

In 1767 Johann Brandmüller, of Friedersthal, near Bethlehem, published *Die täglichen Loosungen der Brüder-Gemeinde fur das Jahr 1767*.

In 1770 Henrich Miller, of Philadelphia, published Augustus Hermann Francke's *The Holy and sure way of Faith of an Evangelical Christian;* German and English on alternate pages. The author was the famous founder of the Halle Orphanage.

---

[1] The first Indian Bible was printed in 1663.

In 1776 the same publisher issued J. A. Freylinghausen's *Ordnung des Heyls, nebst einem Verzeichniss der Wichtigsten Kern-Sprüche der Heiligen Schrift*, etc. Johann Anastasius Freylinghausen (1670–1739) was a renowned theologian and hymn writer of the pietistic school.

In 1787 Leibert and Billmyer, of Germantown, published *Erbauliche Lieder-sammlung.* This hymn-book was published by authority of the Evangelical Lutheran Ministerium of Pennsylvania, compiled mainly by Patriarch Muhlenberg. It superseded the Marburger hymn-book reprints of which had till then been used by the Lutheran congregations of America.

In 1790 Michael Billmeyer, of Germantown, published *Anhang zu dem Gesangbuch der Vereinigten Evangelish-Lutherischen Gemeinen in Nord Amerika.* He also published in the same year *Etliche Christliche Gebete.*

In 1790 Carl Cist, of Philadelphia, published an edition of the Reformed Catechism. 124 pages.

In 1791 Michael Billmeyer published Erasmus Weichenhan's *Christliche Beträchtungen uber die Evangelien*, a quarto of 785 pages, which reflects the religious views of the Schwenkfelders.

In 1793 Michael Billmeyer published Rev. J. H. C. Helmuth's *Betrachtungen der Evangelischen Lehre von der Heiligen Schrift und Taufe; samt einigen Gedanken von den gegenwärtigen Zeiten.* This was followed, in 1795, with a second edition of the Lutheran Hymn Book of 1787.

In 1795 Peter Leibert, of Germantown, issued a new edition of Dr. J. Habermann's *Christliche Morgen- und Abend-gebeter auf alle Tage in der Woche, wie auch Magister Neumann's Kern aller Gebeter und Geistlicher Stundenwecker.*

In 1795, Steiner and Kämmerer, of Philadelphia, published a new Reformed text-book: *Catechismus oder Kurzer Unterricht Christlicher Lehre wie derselbe in denen Reformirten Kirchen und Schulen Deutschlands wie auch in Amerika getrieben wird.*

In 1797, the same firm issued *Das neue und verbesserte Gesang-Buch, worinnen die Psalmen David's samt einer Sammlung alter und neuer Geistreicher Lieder—enthaltent sind. Nebst einem Anhang des Heydelbergischen Catechismus, wie auch erbaulicher Gebäter*, a 12mo. of 766 pages. Heretofore the Reformed Churches of America had been contented with reprints of foreign books (1752, 1753, 1763 and 1772). A synod having been constituted independent of that of Holland in 1793, one of the first steps taken was a resolution to have a new hymn-book compiled, adapted to the needs of Reformed congregations in America.

In 1799, Michael Billmeyer, of Germantown, published a second edition of the Reformed Hymn Book, of the version of 1797.

The list of religious books published in America might be continued, but enough have been cited for our purpose.

The reprint of so many books in this country and the publication of books prepared in America show that there was a demand for the same. Whilst many of the books were used at regular church services, they were also of great benefit to individuals and families in their respective homes. The Bible was read at home, the prayer-book was regularly used and its pages soiled in the course of years showed how highly it was prized, the Catechisms and Sermon books (*Hauspostille* and others) were read at home worship and the hymn-book was the delight of true worshippers. Hymn tunes were often copied for home use. The writer saw not long ago in a book containing in manuscript a sketch of the life of the original owner of the same and his drawings of designs for weaving, also at least fifty melodies with the first verses of as many hymns for use in the family. The reading of God's word and the prayers of the prayer-book, the singing of hymns, the reading of the sermons in the sermon-book, and the recital of the Catechism strengthened the pioneer and his descendants in their faith, quickened them in their walks in the truth and comforted them in their trials of life in this new world. The influence of religion in the home is forcibly illustrated in the life of Regina the captive. After her return to her home, her mother and she visited Patriarch Muhlenberg, who gives in the Hallische Nachrichten, an extended account of her capture, her life among the Indians, her surrender by the Indians and her remarkable experience, when brought with other captives to Carlisle, a town in the Cumberland Valley in Pennsylvania and her remarkable restoration to her mother. The account shows that home religion had a wonderful influence on Regina and sustained her during the years of her captivity. The simple repetition of the first lines of two hymns *Jesum lieb ich ewiglich*, etc., and *Allein und doch nicht ganz allein bin ich in meiner Einsamkeit*, etc., by the distressed mother, who had failed to recognize her daughter among the returned captives, was followed by the daughter's recognition of her mother. The mutual embrace of mother and daughter that affected the hearts of all the witnesses, has been the story always heard with gratitude to God for the power of religion in

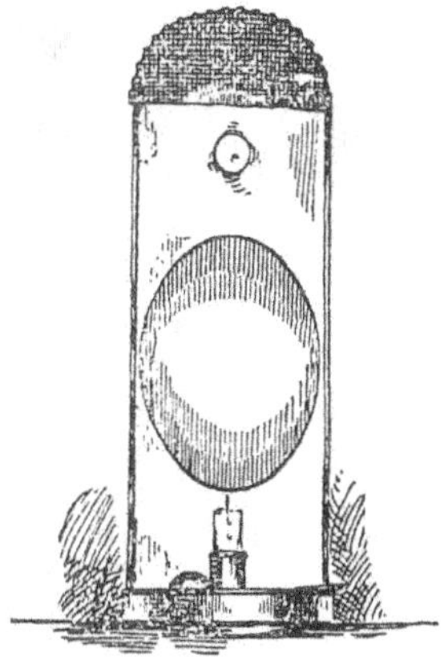

Sconce used in churches in Lancaster county.

the domestic life of the pioneer. Regina's wish to have a copy of the Bible and a hymn-book for herself was gratified by Patriarch Muhlenberg who presented a copy of the Bible to her and furnished her money to buy a hymn-book. The Christian homes were the places where, before the erection of churches and school houses, the first ministers of the Gospel were welcomed to hold services. The house, the barn, the grove and the forest were the places where the pioneers gathered, hungry for the preaching of the Gospel and where ministers preached the word and administered the Sacraments and the people united in prayer and the praise of God.

Illustration from an old reader.

CHAPTER VII.

Care of Children.

Wappen von Krefeld.

A MOST important part of the domestic life of the pioneer and his descendants was the care of their children. The Psalmist of old wrote, "Lo, children are an heritage of the Lord, and the fruit of the womb is his reward. As arrows are in the hand of a mighty man: so are children of the youth. Happy is the man that hath his quiver full of them: they shall not be ashamed, but they shall speak with the enemies in the gate" (Ps. 127: 3–5). The Apostle Paul wrote, "But if any provide not for his own, and specially for those of his own house, he hath denied the faith and is worse than an infidel" (1 Tim. 5: 8). The records of baptism kept by pastors and the entries of births and baptisms in the family Bibles show that Pennsylvania-Germans often had large families of children.

The care of children required the proper supply of their bodily wants. Parents labored diligently that the home might be well supplied with food, and this was freely given at the appointed meals and at other times when children asked for food. Children of the former century were taught how to behave at the table. The model schoolmaster, Christopher Dock, considered it a part of his work to teach children rules for good behavior at home as well as in the school and in the church.

Prayers at meals taught children that their daily bread came from the Giver of all good gifts. Parents also supplied their children with clothing, suitable for wearing in the different seasons of the year. They taught them the proper care of garments, that there might be no sinful waste. Parents provided comfortable beds for their offspring, that they might not suffer from cold in the days in which houses were without furnaces in cellars, and without hot-water and steam-heating plants. At the time when the services of a doctor of medicine could not easily be secured, a supply of remedies secured from the barnyard, the garden, the orchard, the meadow and the forest was kept on hand for prompt use in days of sickness.

Parents also cared for the mental training of their children. They were anxious for the schoolhouse as well as the church, for the schoolmaster as well as the pastor. The family sustained a close relation to the schoolmaster, who was often entertained by families whose children were his pupils. Children were not merely sent to school and their entire mental training left to the schoolmaster. Parents assisted their children in learning their lessons at home, and when schools and schoolmasters were wanting parents were the teachers of their children. Such home instruction, though often very limited, showed the interest of parents in the welfare of their children. When this was neglected the young grew up very ignorant and were in a most deplorable condition, as is evident from the testimony of Patriarch Muhlenberg and others, who in their first labors in this country were not only pastors, but also teachers and had adults advanced in years in schools attended by children. The German A B C Book and Spelling Book were frequently printed in this country, also Arithmetics, Readers, including the New Testament, Psalter and other books. The Catechism and Hymn-Book were also used in teaching the young to read. In many homes children would gather in the long winter evening at the table, at which meals were served during the day, that parents might assist them in learning their lessons. Some years ago the writer had as a parishioner an aged mother, a daughter of Jaebez Weiser, a descendant of Conrad Weiser, who told him of the customs that prevailed in her youth, which was that children gathered around the table in the evening, and were assisted by adults in learning their lessons, and were taught passages of Scripture and hymns, and that such had been the custom of her ancestors.

Parents also cared for the spiritual wants of their children. They presented them for baptism at an early day, as is evident from the old church records and pastors' private journals. Parents read God's Word, prayed and praised God not only for their own growth in grace, but also for the spiritual blessing of their children. Children were early taught God's word and were also taught to pray. The Catechism was taught by the head of the family and at a proper age children received further instruction in the parochial school and in due time were instructed by the pastor and learned the Catechism, Bible History, prayers and hymns to be prepared for confirmation. Parents encouraged them at home in learning the lessons assigned them. Parents encouraged their children to attend church services and were not ashamed to have them accompany them to and from God's House. The writer recalls the fact that nearly sixty years ago he sat by the side of his father in an old church, the floor of which was of bricks, and in which there were movable plain benches with backs. Home care for the spiritual welfare of children led them early to think of God, of sin, of Christ the blessed Savior, of the forgiveness of sin, of the Holy Ghost—the new heart and holy life—of hell and the punishment of sin—of Heaven and eternal glory. Children thus trained were given to the fear, love and service of God.

Parents also cared for their children by the right use of Solomon's rod. Because they loved their children and desired them to grow up to be godly men and women, they were faithful in instructing them and did what they could by word and prayer for their improvement. But when children would be disobedient or were guilty of wicked deeds, parents did not hesitate to use the rod, and its proper application resulted in saving many a child from continuance in wickedness and brought them to earnest thought and a change of life. Lasting impressions were made upon some who are still living, by the use of a mother's slipper and rod. The writer heard the Rev. Dr. Christlieb state in an address at the meeting of the Evangelical Alliance in New York in 1873, that he missed two things in America that he still found in Germany: the one was the poor by the side of the rich in the churches, and the second was Solomon's rod in the home. He said that in Germany the rod was still used and that their youth became *Kräftige Bengel.* Dr. Christlieb visited the great cities along and not far from the Atlantic Coast. Had he come to Falkner Swamp in Montgomery County, to the Bushkill and Monocacy in Northampton, to the Jordan and Cedar Creek in Lehigh, to the Moselem and Tulpehocken in Berks, to the Swatara and Quitopahilla in Lebanon, to the Cocalico and the Conestoga in Lancaster, the Conewago and the Kreutz Krick in York and the Conococheague in Adams and Franklin Counties, he would have found the rich and the poor together in the churches and that Solomon's rod was still in active use in many homes.

The children of our ancestors were taught early in life to work. Parents assigned such labors as their children could perform. Thus boys and girls had their daily duties, and they were expected to discharge them faithfully and properly. As they grew up to be men and women they were fitted for life's work. The sons and daughters were prepared to take the places of their parents. No one thought it a disgrace to work on a farm or to learn a trade. They were proud of their ability to labor.

The young were allowed proper recreations. They had their games in the house, in the yard, at the barn, on the field, in the meadow and in the forest. Happy days were spent by the young people of neighbors meeting successively at their respective homes. Aged parents witnessed with pleasure the young in their various games, and cheerfully furnished refreshments on such occasions. Homes were made attractive by proper privileges granted by parents. The homes where the young were permitted to have enjoyments suited to their age are ever remembered with pleasure.

That Pennsylvania-Germans favor education is evident from the existence of the parochial schoolhouse soon after the first settlements, the schoolhouse in more limited districts, the private schools established in still more limited sections, the academy, the seminary, the public school, the normal schools, and colleges and universities of the present century and the large number of German names on the rolls of schools and in the catalogues of the many institutions of our State.

Cover of Sauer Almanac for 1776, *Troublous Times*, one-half size.

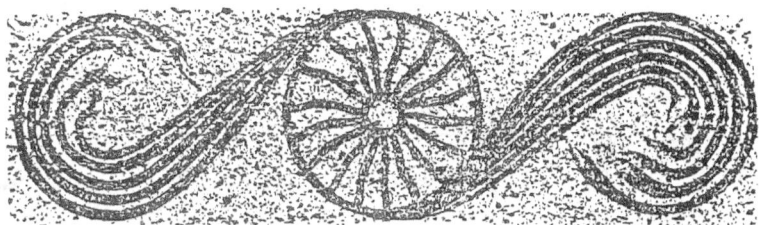

CHAPTER VIII.

SERVANTS.

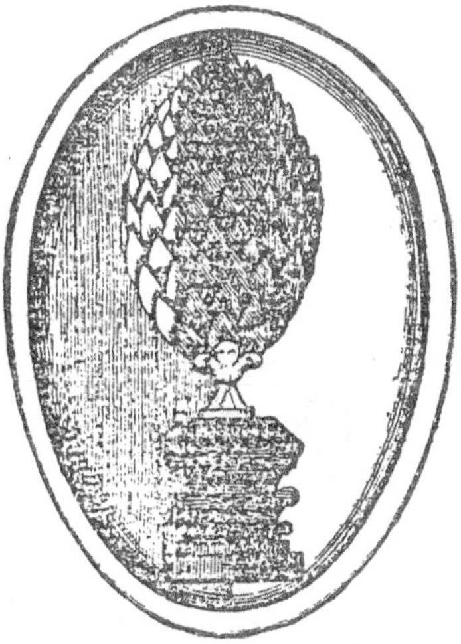

Arms of Augsburg.

ANOTHER important feature of the domestic life of our ancestors and their descendants was the attention that was shown to servants. Pennsylvania at a very early day opposed slavery. Servant labor was necessary in many homes. Servants were usually well cared for. Their treatment depended on the character of the masters and also on the conduct of the servants. There were cruel masters and there were unfaithful servants. There were many kind-hearted masters and mistresses who took a deep interest in the welfare of those employed by them. Such was the case even with the redemptioners,[1] who had German masters. Many have heard the story of the redemptioner, whose request that the contract with his master should contain the provision that he was to have meat twice in each week, was cheerfully granted. Upon arrival at the mas-

[1] A class of indentured servants confined chiefly to Pennsylvania.

ter's home, the redemptioner had meat at supper, his first meal. When meat was given also at breakfast on the following morning, his face was filled with sadness. The master asked why he looked so sad, the answer was that it was true that the contract stated that he should have meat twice in each week, but he did not expect to receive meats at two meals so near together. So great was his surprise when told that he had no reason to be sad for he would have meat served him at three meals on each day that he exclaimed that he wished that his back were also a stomach!

Servants were allowed on ordinary occasions to be seated at the table with the family at meals. Their wants were as abundantly supplied as those of the children of the home. They had comfortable beds and were allowed sufficient time for proper rest after the labors of the day. They were expected to work, for they were not employed simply to be witnesses of the diligence of the master and the mistress. When they labored faithfully they were commended, and when they were indolent they were reproved. The faithful servant was loved by the master and well cared for in times of sickness. In a home where God was feared and religion was a saving power, servants were also blest by its influence. The God-fearing master and mistress by word and deed made lasting impressions on those whom they employed. A strong mutual attachment was often formed by masters and servants. The servant frequently showed the love of a son or daughter and the master and mistress the love of parents. Those who served whilst young were fitted like children of the family for life's earnest duties. Separations were often marked by mutual regrets and friendship cherished throughout life by those who were once related as masters and servants.

The question has often been asked why Pennsylvania-Germans are able to retain servants for a much longer period of time than others. It is entirely owing to the treatment which masters and mistresses give their servants. The latter have bodies and souls as well as the former. When this fact is duly recognized, those who employ servants will treat servants as those who with them may be ultimately heirs and joint heirs with Him who declared that the greatest is he who serves. The writer's paternal ancestor was a redemptioner, and a recent examination of an old church record shows the friendly relation that existed a hundred years ago between the family of the writer's ancestor and the family of the one in whose service the redemptioner had been for many years.

From Sauer almanac.

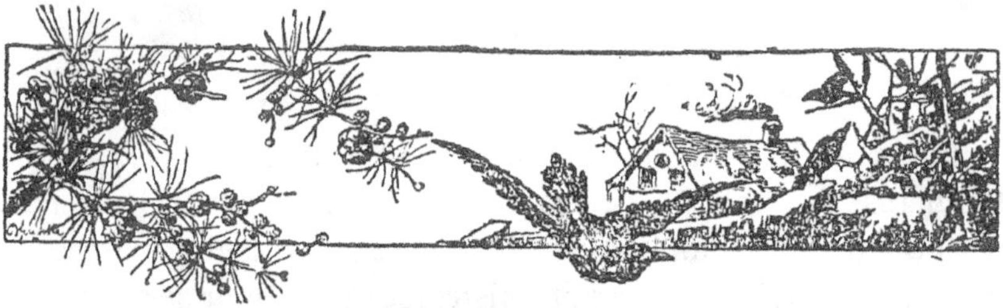

CHAPTER IX.

The Aged and Infirm.

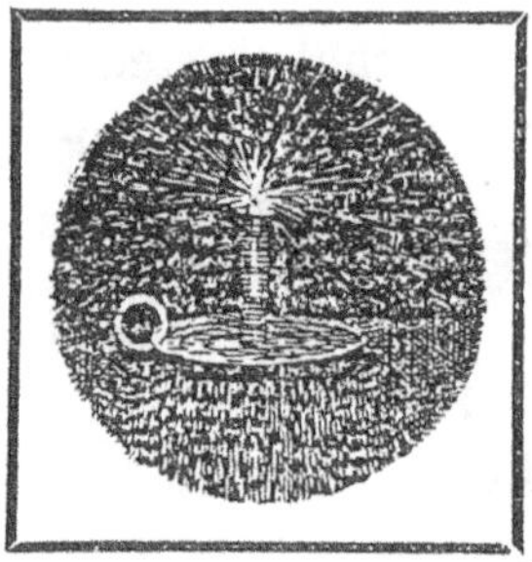

TO the history of the domestic life of ancestors belongs also the attention that was given aged and infirm parents and grandparents. Memory ever recalls with pleasure the love that was shown to those who could no longer labor as in earlier years. A part of the home was specially assigned to aged parents or grandparents in which they could spend their declining years in peace. Their bodily wants were faithfully supplied. After the labors of the day were ended by those who could toil, it was considered a great privilege to cheer the aged. Sometimes a separate dwelling was erected for the aged and their home was eagerly sought by their descendants. Often a faithful unmarried daughter considered it a duty to remain with the aged father or mother to the end of their life. The home of the aged had limited but sufficient dimensions to make them comfortable. The plain furniture of the living room included stove, wood-chest, tables, chairs, corner cupboard, clock, shelving for the Bible, prayer-book, hymn-book and book of sermons. The bedroom contained bed with canopy and vallence, wash-stand, looking-glass, desk, high chest of drawers, wardrobe, large arm chair or rocking chair, and a few quaint pictures on the wall.

Blessed hours were spent with the aged, who loved to recall events of their earlier years but also loved to hear their offspring tell of their daily experiences. Valuable lessons were taught by the aged. Their counsel was always for the welfare of the young, whose future course in life was often determined by the influence exerted in the home of the aged. What a blessed retreat for those who experienced many of life's trials and sorrows. Here they could unburden their minds and hearts without fear of abuse, here they found sincere sympathy and heard words of genuine comfort, here they received good counsel to correct errors in life, to restore peace between those who needed reconciliation, to prevent entrance upon engagements that would bring nothing but ruin.

No man or woman has ever had occasion to regret the attention shown to the aged and infirm. A mother's prayer and a father's blessing are rich legacies, that cheer men in life's arduous duties, that make better men and women here and help in directing their thoughts to and fitting them for the eternal home in the kingdom of glory on high, in the Father's home of many mansions. God's commandment: "Honor thy Father and Mother, that thy days may be long upon the land which the Lord thy God giveth thee"—contains not only a commandment but also a promise. Wise are they who profit by heeding the explanation given by the great reformer, "We should so fear and love God as not to despise and displease our parents and superiors, but honor, serve, obey, love and esteem them."

CHAPTER X.

Hospitality.

HOSPITALITY was ever shown in the genuine Pennsylvania-German home. The man who had occasion to ask for food and shelter was kindly received and his wants were cheerfully supplied. "God reward you for your kindness" was the expression of the gratitude of many whose hunger had been supplied and who had peaceful slumbers when they were permitted to rest without fear of harm.

Unexpected visitors were not permitted to think that they were not welcome. Their arrival was cheered by hearty greetings. The horse was speedily stabled and the host and guests were soon in the best room in the house and engaged in pleasant and profitable conversation. The good housewife and her aids attended to the preparation of the meals to be served. Nothing was too good to be given to visitors. Whilst an apology might be offered that for the want of time the preparation was not as ample as it would have been if the coming of the visitors had been known, there was always an abundance of good food. Intervals between meals were hours of most delightful entertainment. Visitors were pressed to remain during the night and when they consented to do so, the evening was spent in a cheerful and profitable manner.

When, however, visitors had previously announced their coming or had accepted an invitation to visit, extensive preparations were made for their reception and entertain-

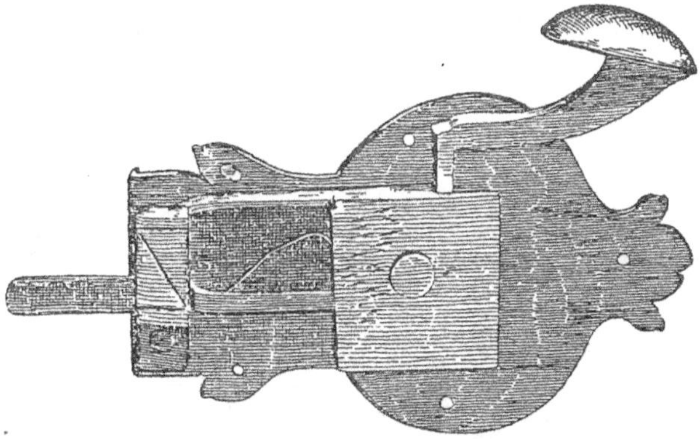

Wrought-iron door lock and latch.

ment. The house, the porches, the walks in the yard adjoining the house, the barn and its yard received special attention. The day preceding the arrival of visitors was a very busy day for the housewife and her aids. An abundance of food was made ready for the occasion. All of the family arose early on the appointed day. The house was set in order, children were neatly dressed and adults also wore better clothing than on working days. The arrival of guests was anxiously awaited and their coming was speedily announced by the one who first saw their approach. All special work had been declared off during the stay of the visitors and the time was given to their best entertainment. They were kindly greeted upon their arrival and their entire stay was made as agreeable as possible. Conversation seldom flagged and for a change the garden, the orchard, the meadow, the fields under cultivation, the spring house, the barn, the sheds and often even the different rooms in the house were shown to visitors. At the table there was the best evidence of special preparation by the good mother and her helps, and after grace was said, there was the special word to the visitors to feel at home, to help themselves and eat heartily. The hospitality that was shown was genuine. It strengthened the bonds of friendship and added to the happiness of those who had many experiences in life of a different nature. By such entertainment they were cheered to labor with greater diligence and patience, knowing that human life has also a bright side.

Der
Hoch-Deutsch-
Americanische
Calender,
Auf das Jahr
Nach der Gnadenreichen Geburt unsers
HErrn und Heylandes JEsu Christi
1776.
(Welches ein Schalt-Jahr von 366 Tagen ist.)
In sich haltende: Die Wochen-Tage; den Tag des Monats; Tage welche bemerkt werden; des Monds Auf- und Niedergang; des Monds Zeichen und Grad: des Monds Viertel: Aspecten der Planeten, sammt der Witterung; Des 7 Gestirns Aufgang, Süd-Platz und Untergang; Der Sonnen Auf- und Untergang; Der Venus, (des Morgen- oder Abend-Sterns) Auf- und Untergang. Nebst verschiedenen andern Berichten; Erklärung der Zeichen, Aderlaß-Täflein, Anzeigung der Finsternisse, Couten, Faren, &c. &c.
Eingerichtet vor 40 Grad Norder-Breite, sonderlich vor Pennsylvanien;
Jedoch in denen angrenzenden Landen ohne mercklichen Unterschied zu gebrauchen.
Der regierende Planet vor dieses Jahr ist ♄
Güldene Zahl 10 | Sonnen-Cirkel 21
Epacten 9 | Sonntags Buchstab G F
Zum acht und dreyßigsten mal heraus gegeben.

Germantown: Gedruckt und zu finden bey Christoph Saur.
Auch können die auswärtige Krämer solche bey Mr. Reinbold und der Wittwe Dezin, in Philadelphia haben, oder in Lancäster bey Ludwig Laumann, in Neuyorck bey Michel Hoffmann, u. andern.

Title page of Sauer Almanac for 1776, one-half size.

CHAPTER XI.

Special Occasions.

Arms of Pastorius family.

THE domestic life of the pioneer was frequently brightened by special occasions which were not alone of interest to the family but to neighbors and friends as well.

The baptism of children took place in churches as soon as such were erected. Old records of pastors and of congregations often give the reason for baptism in private houses. The records give not only the names of the parents, the name of the child, the date of birth and the date of baptism, but also the names of the sponsors, the number of which varied from one to six or even more.

After the baptism of a child the friends gathered in the home of the parents and partook of a rich provision for the festive occasion. Certificates of baptism were carefully preserved. The relation of the sponsor to the child baptized was often very close. The character of the sponsor was often effective in determining that of the child.

MARRIAGES took place, after the bans had been called thrice in the church, in the church building itself or at the pastor's residence, at the home of the bride and occasionally at the office of the magistrate in cases where a license was first procured from the Governor. Wedding feasts were usually well attended. Rich provisions had been made for the same. Whilst for the aged they were days of pleasant reunions, for the young they were days of great merriment and at times of excesses that were not to be commended. Wedding trips to distant places were not then in fashion. At times when the conveniences of travel were very limited, the wedding party, for the want of suitable conveyances, proceeded to the church or pastor's residence on horseback.

THE death of a member of the family brought a sad experience to all the members of the same. Prompt attention was given to the preparation of the body for burial. Frequently the body was laid on a strip of sod. Watchers spent the nights preceding the burial in the house of mourning. Due notice of the date of burial and invitations to the funeral were given by sending out a number of messengers, who requested those whom they met to extend the notice and invitation to others. Extensive preparations were made for the entertainment of attendants at the funeral, who often came from distant places. Funerals were generally numerously attended. Before the beginning of the service at the house, refreshments were offered to attendants. The custom was to hand cake and wine to all. The service at the house was frequently held outside of the house after the coffin had been brought from the house and placed on chairs and the mourners gathered around the same. The service included a hymn, a short address and a prayer. After this service the coffin was placed on a wagon or sled (before the regular hearse was used), and the procession was formed to accompany the remains to "God's acre" near the church, and in the days when carriages and other conveyances were not over abundant and many rode on horses, frequently the wife was seated on a pillion in the rear of the rider. On arrival at the burial ground the coffin was placed on a bier, the lid of the coffin was removed and the remains viewed for the last time. As soon as the coffin lid was replaced and fastened, a hymn was begun and frequently the pastor and cantor at once moved and led the procession towards the grave, singing until the grave was reached. After the coffin was deposited in the grave the regular burial service was conducted by the pastor, and frequently all remained until the pall-bearers, who in early days also made the grave, had filled the grave with ground. The minister was always expected to preach a funeral sermon whether the burial took place in God's acre near the church, or in a private burial ground near the home of the deceased. When the burial took place in God's acre near the church, the service including sermon was held in the church. When the burial was on a private burial ground the sermon was often preached in a barn. Frequently the text of the funeral sermon had been selected by the deceased long before his or her death. The funeral sermon was of great importance in the early days when there was not as frequent preaching as in later periods. Then the minister's service was not simply to comfort the sorrowing, but also to benefit all others by a faithful presentation of the divine word. After the service in church or other place and burial the mourners and other attendants returned to the house of mourning to partake of the funeral feast. This custom was regularly observed.

There were, however, many abuses connected with serving cake and drinks before the service at the house and the funeral feast after the burial. No one wished to be charged with a miserly spirit or a lack of consideration for the wants of those who came great distances to attend the funeral service.

The writer knew in his childhood a minister, who put an end to the first custom in his parish in a heroic way. When the bottle containing drink was handed to him he took the bottle and dashed it to the ground. After the pastor's most decided disapproval the custom was no longer observed by his people. Another minister who had occasion to bury a person who had been supported by a township, embraced the opportunity of expressing his disapproval of the funeral feast by announcing, after he had read the sketch of the life of the deceased, "Die Zubereitung ist nicht grosz, die Zubereitung ist nicht grosz, doch können die Grabmacher und das Gefress mit nach Haus gehen."

AMONG other special occasions that brought changes into the experience of families, we may mention the erection of buildings. The necessary excavation was often made with the help of neighbors, who gathered on an appointed day or days and by their combined labors not only executed the work in a short time, but also by their kindness placed their neighbor under obligations to them and strengthened the bond of union between them. The family that was able to give proper refreshments to those who thus favored it, was sure to secure for itself an unenviable reputation by neglecting to provide abundantly for such an occasion. In one of our eastern counties a village bore for a long time and may bear yet the name of Crackersport—a name given to it, it is said, to commemorate the fact that one of its inhabitants, who had been kindly served by his neighbors by making the necessary excavation for a building, served refreshments in the form of crackers.

After the necessary preparation of timber, another day of kind neighborly service was that of log raising. The framing of a house or barn was hard and dangerous work, but was accomplished by the combined services of men who had willing hearts and strong arms. Such occasions were often days of merriment as well as labor for the participants. The best of food and the best of drinks were freely furnished by those who appreciated the aid rendered by neighbors.

AN occasion of light work and much merriment was that of apple paring and cutting and boiling applebutter. The family itself was expected to attend to cider-making and apple-gathering before the day on which neighbors assembled to assist in special work. Apple paring and cutting were marked by much merriment. Old and new stories were told—and popular songs were heartily rendered. The boiling of cider, the addition of divided apples and the necessary stirring required careful attention. But as the number of persons assembled was always much larger than the number at work during the boiling of the cider and the apples—those, who awaited their turn at work, found time to engage in games that were common in those days and thus the night was spent in merrymaking as well as work. A member of the Lebanon County Historical Society, who is also a member of the Pennsylvania-German Society, some time ago read a paper upon "The Cider Press and Applebutter Making," before the County Society, a most valuable addition to the domestic history of our ancestors.

CORN-HUSKING was regularly attended to by families, who were kindly aided by their neighbors. It was often a night work on the floor of a barn or another building. The dimly lighted place was not only the scene of faithful work, but also of much merriment. When the work was ended games of various kinds were indulged in and an abundance of refreshments partaken of.

ON butchering days families were also assisted by their neighbors. The killing and dressing of the cattle took place on the preceding day. On butchering day fires were started early and breakfast served before sunrise. The killing of swine was promptly followed by the scalding, scraping, cleansing, dressing and quartering of the same. The cleaning of entrails, the preparation of hams and shoulders, the rendering of lard and tallow, the chopping of meats and the making of sausage, the boiling of meats and the making of liver sausage, the preparation of meats for the brining tubs and the smoke-house kept all busy to the approach of evening and often to a late hour in the night. On butchering day no one suffered hunger or thirst. Breakfast was a full meal. At dinner often the largest turkey was served, with an abundance of other dishes. At supper the new sausage was usually a part of the meal. When the neighbors left for their homes they carried samples of the new sausage and pudding for themselves and those who had remained at home.

FOR a long time our ancestors had no carpets in their houses and their beds were without the quilts that became so common among later generations. Thus, carpet-rag-parties and quilting-parties followed in later years. They both helped to make the history of the Pennsylvania-

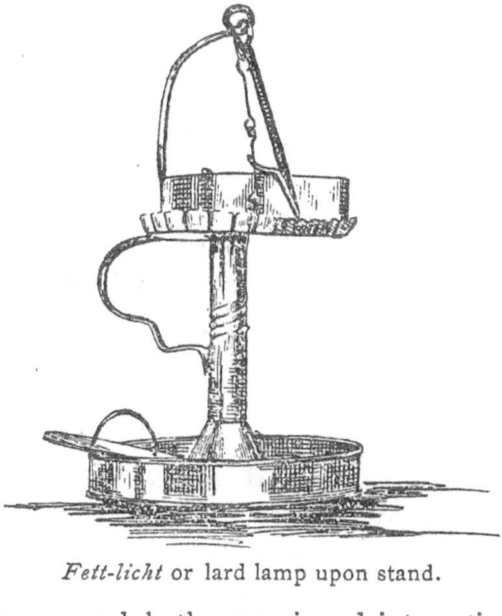

Fett-licht or lard lamp upon stand.

German homes and both occasioned interesting events in the life of the family. They were occasions on which the mothers and daughters of a neighborhood gathered in a house to assist the mother and daughters of the same. Whilst rags were carefully sewed for the carpet and the materials stretched on the frame quilted according to the pattern traced on the goods, many revelations were made touching life in the different families represented on such occasions and also in families not represented. The participants heard on a single day the news of months and years. If any felt inclined to report what they had heard, and were asked what authority they had for what they said, they cited the carpet-rag or quilting party. The good housewife would invariably serve good food, including excellent tea, and none of her friends had occasion to complain of a want of liberality.

A PUBLIC sale or vendue was also a special experience of the family leading a quiet life. Before the day of sale extensive preparations were made in arranging the articles to be sold. A large quantity of food was provided—not only for the men engaged to conduct the sale and specially invited friends, but also for those whose chief interest at a vendue was a good square meal. When the appointed time for the sale arrived, the reading of the conditions of the sale was often a very ceremonious act. The crier of the sale held an important position. His praise of the articles offered for sale was to cause high bidding, his pleasantries were to entertain the people assembled and the faithful use of his strong voice was to increase his reputation as a crier. Parties not specially interested in the purchase of goods found the public sale a favorable occasion for the transaction of private business. The scandal-monger embraced the opportunity to spread injurious reports concerning his neighbor. The politician also made use of the occasion by trying to secure votes for himself. The young people found parts of the house, the yard, the barn, the barnyard, the orchard and the fields good places for their games. The huckster with his hot soup and a variety of cakes was also present and usually well patronized. Enemies who met at public sales would often engage in bodily conflicts, and their shedding of blood was of interest to themselves and to those who witnessed their bloody combat.

Kitchen utensils, carving knife and fork, ladles, skimmer and cake turner.

An appeal to a magistrate after such a conflict at a public sale or at a gathering of people on an occasion of a different character, was not always followed by the prompt issue of a warrant for the arrest of the party against whom the complaint was made. A magistrate of nearly a hundred years ago was asked by a party, who had been whipped in a fight, for a warrant for the arrest of his opponent. The magistrate answered that the appellant ought to be ashamed that he allowed the other party to whip him, that the appellant could whip the other party, if he but tried rightly to do so. The words of the magistrate inspired the appellant with courage, and he whipped the previous victor, who after his defeat also appealed to the magistrate, who commanded the vanquished victor to leave promptly, as the other party had already applied for his service. Of a magistrate of a still earlier period it was said, that he would at times take parties, who appeared before him as plaintiff

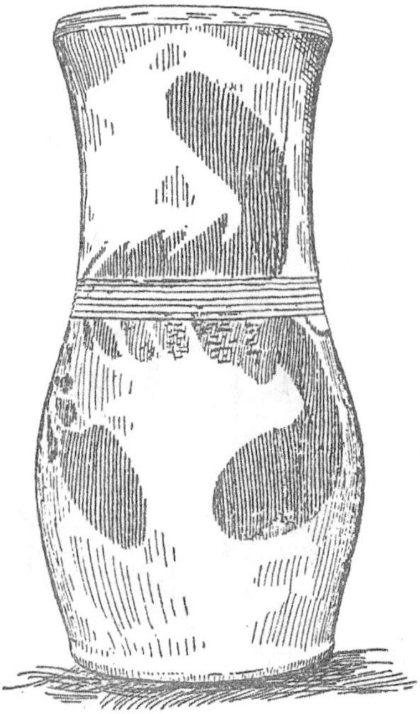

Specimen of early Pennsylvania-German pottery.

Calabash or gourd dipper.

and defendant, from his office to a back yard to settle their disputes by a bodily conflict. He was, however, not a Pennsylvania-German.

ANOTHER special occasion in the home life of our ancestors was caused by a change of residence. When the new home was not at a great distance from the old, moving was often quietly attended to by the aid of a few neighbors, who on successive days assisted in removing the effects of a family to their new home. But when the removal required a journey of 10, 15, 20 or more miles and all the effects were to be carried to the new residence on the same day, then great preparations were necessary before moving day. An abundance of food was prepared and carefully packed to be carried securely. On the day and night preceding moving day neighbors arrived with their large wagons, on which household goods and farm utensils were safely packed. The journey was begun as

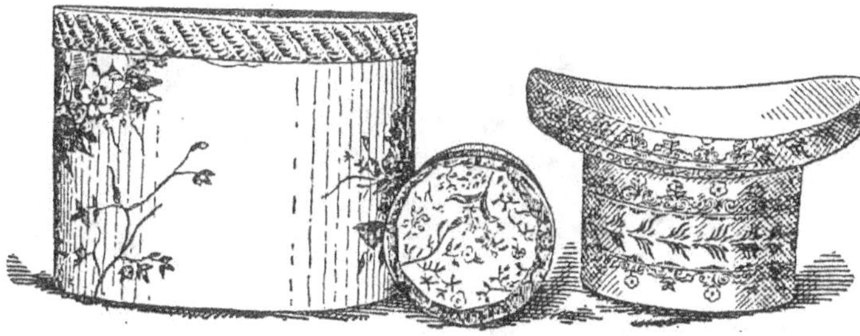

Typical Pennsylvania-German traveling outfit, the large box for the wife's bonnet.

early as possible on moving day. A day without rain was the cause of great joy, and a day with rain brought many regrets. The journey itself was often accompanied with incidents of interest, but at times also with accidents not soon forgotten. The safe arrival at the new home was followed by work of busy hands in unloading goods and placing effects in the house and other buildings. The first meal in the new home was made of the abundant supply that was brought from the old. When the neighbors from the old home were obliged to tarry for a night before returning, and the neighbors of the new home visited the newly arrived family there was a social gathering in the new home, to be remembered long by all participants. When, however, the change of residence required a long journey from some part in eastern Pennsylvania to a place in a central or western county or possibly in a county on the western border of the State, then a family had a still greater variety of experiences. All the articles that could not well be carried on the journey were sold privately or at a public sale. Large covered wagons were secured for packing and carrying the heavier goods to be removed. Other covered wagons were necessary for carrying lighter goods and provisions for the journey. Whilst

German immigrants crossing the Alleghanies.

often places were found in wagons already named for those who made the journey, special conveyances were at times provided for the family and friends. When a number of families moved at the same time and to the same region of country, the journey was marked by increased interest. At meal times the caravan would halt, fires were kindled by the side of the road, or in the forest, and food was carefully prepared and served abundantly. Horses were supplied with provender and allowed to graze. When the night had to be spent where no lodging could be secured, the pilgrims slept in their wagons. During the past summer the writer met a number of very aged persons in a county on the western border of our State, who in the thirties of the closing century made such a journey from an eastern county to the county in which the writer met them. The company who made the journey numbered between thirty and forty persons and had varied experiences, including the following: One day the company felt glad to learn that lodging for the night could be secured in a hotel located at the foot of a mountain. They were, however, surprised when they reached the hotel to find that the house had only one large room with a bar at one end. Bedding was brought from the wagons and laid on the floor of the one room. Here the entire number of pilgrims slept during the night. In the morning they were surprised to find the landlord and his wife rising from behind the bar. Whether they had slept there during the night or watched their supply of liquors was not stated. Such a moving and location in a new place was a new period in the life of a family. To trace the history of a single family would often require a volume. The writer, by special invitation, attended several reunions of the Bortz family in Mercer county, which were attended by many claiming relationship. He also, by special request, attended a reunion of the Gangaware family in Westmoreland county. The ancestors of both families moved from Lehigh county, formerly part of Northampton county, to these western counties. Last summer the Lichtenwallner family held their first reunion at Allentown. They all descended from Johannes Lichtenwallner, who came to America in 1733 and settled in Lehigh county. The intensely interesting history of the family, published since the reunion—shows not only the large number of descendants in Pennsylvania, but also the large number of persons descended from the Ohio branch of the family. By removals from eastern and central Pennsylvania, Pennsylvania-German families became important factors in the settlement of territories beyond the borders of our State and in the making of other States of our glorious Union.

Der Neue, Gemeinnützige

Landwirthschafts Calender,

Auf das Jahr, nach der heilbringenden Geburt unsers HErrn JEsu Christi,

1802.

Welches ein gemeines Jahr von 365 Tagen ist.

Darinnen, nebst richtiger Festrechnung, die Sonn- und Monds-Finsternisse, des Monds Gestalt und Viertel, Monds-Aufgang, Monds-Zeichen, Aspecten der Planeten und Witterung, Sonnen Auf- und Untergang, des Siebengestirns Aufgang, Südplatz und Untergang, der Venus Auf- und Untergang, das hohe Wasser zu Philadelphia, Courten, Fairs, und andere zu einem Calender gehörige Sachen zu finden.

Imgleichen, lehrreiche und unterhaltende Geschichten, &c.

Mit sonderbarem Fleiß nach dem Pennsylvanischen und der angrenzenden Staaten Horizont und Nordhöhe berechnet.

Zum Funfzehntenmal herausgegeben.

Lancäster, Gedruckt und zu haben bey Johann Albrecht, in der neuen Buchdruckerey, in der Prinz-strasse, das 2te Haus, nördlich vom Gefängniß.

Title page of Pennsylvania-German Farmers' Almanac.

CHAPTER XII.

Characteristics of the Pennsylvania–German Pioneer.

INTRODUCTION of sin into the world affected the relation of man to the Superior Being, his relation to his fellowmen and his own private life. The separation of man from God left him in darkness and all his own devised ways fail to restore him to the relation he first sustained to God. Sin has made man extremely selfish and cruel in his relation to his fellowmen, hence the deeds of violence, the acts of base abuse of sexual relations, the deeds of dishonesty and fraud in dealing with others, the untruthfulness in his associations with others and the constant manifestation of the evil desires for the property and the associates of his neighbors, and, in his private life, the abuse of God's good gifts, hence a life of intemperance, a life of lewdness, a life worse than that of the brute creation.

The Christian religion is not only to restore the right relation of man to the Superior Being, but also to effect a proper relation of man to man and to affect his own private life. St. Paul, the great Apostle, wrote, "The grace of God that bringeth salvation hath appeared to all men, teaching us that, denying ungodliness and worldly lusts, we should live soberly, righteously and godly in this present world: Looking for that blessed hope, and the glorious appearance of the great God and our Saviour Jesus Christ; who gave himself for us, that he might redeem us from all iniquity, and purify unto himself a peculiar people, zealous of good works."

Not all Pennsylvania-German pioneers were good Christian people. With such as were not, sin did abound, and men were given to idolatry, giving to the creature what is to be given to God only; they abused God's name by profanity, by superstitious practices, by lying and deceiving by the same; they cared not for God's day, God's house and God's word; the right relation between parents and children was wanting; they hesitated not in doing bodily harm to their neighbors; they were given to all grades of sins of the flesh; they made light of untruthfulness and were given to many evil deeds which evidenced the covetousness of their depraved hearts.

Of the great number of pioneers, whose minds were enlightened by the word of God and whose hearts were under the influence of His grace, it could be said that they feared, loved and trusted in God above all things. When vessels that bore them to this country encountered storms, there was a marked difference between immigrants who feared, loved and trusted in God and those who were the very opposite of God's people. Those who were ungodly were filled with despair, and those in fellowship with God, manifested their trust in Him, by their prayers and hymns and humble submission to His dealing with them. Upon arrival in this country and when beginning their new homes in this new world, they asked God to bless their work, and often in the erection of a building, they showed their trust in God, by placing a stone in the wall of the building, bearing an inscription which showed their confidence in the most High and asking Him to bless their home.

An Ephrata pilgrim.

God's name was dear to them and they made use of it in every time of need and in daily prayers, praise and thanksgiving, hence their desire to have God's word, the hymn-book and the prayer-book to aid them in their devotions.

The Lord's-day was properly kept, the people frequented the sanctuary and joined reverently in the right worship of the most High and received with gladness the message of salvation. The remaining hours of the Lord's-day were precious to them, giving them time for home worship and private devotion. The work necessary on the Lord's-day was performed in the most quiet way and the home was marked by true devotion on the part of its occupants.

The pioneer was characterized by a strong love for home. His ambition was to have a house for himself and family. For this he labored and happy was he when he had secured it. He also had a great love for his household. He prized his godly wife and loved his children and did not murmur when their number was increased. But not only did parents love their home and children, the latter also loved their home and their parents and other members of the family. Harbaugh's *Heimweh* shows the influence of parental piety and right care of children and the longings that are awakened in those who profited by having godly parents and a good home.

The good pioneer was characterized by a proper regard for human life. Murder and suicide were to him great sins. When he witnessed or heard of either he was shocked. Not only did he regard the preservation of his own life a great duty, but also the prevention of harm to others and the assistance of all who were in want.

The old church records contain the entries of the birth and baptism of children.. The fact that they faithfully state the illegitimate birth of children shows that there was no inclination to hide the sins of the people. The fact, however, that the number of illegitimate births was small compared with the number born in wedlock, shows plainly the regard which pioneers had for the state of matrimony. Adultery was a grievous sin to them. Divorces were abhorred by them. Parents counselled their children to lead pure lives and gave them good advice concerning the choice of a husband or a wife.

The godly pioneer had a high regard for man's right to what God granted him of earthly possessions. Not all that men have is held by them—with God's approval. Men have a right to call their own what they have secured by godly labor, by economy void of covetousness, by inheritance, or by gift. Robbery, thieving and fraud are all condemned by "thou shalt not steal." Pioneers taught their children not to steal, but to labor with their hands—that they might have to give to him that needeth. Dishonesty in children was severely punished. Honesty in all dealings was encouraged and constantly commended. A promise to pay was a solemn obligation of which God was a witness—and in His fear it was promptly met.

Truthfulness is important in all the relations of men—not only in the more extended circles in life—but also in the quiet home. No wonder that the pioneer prized it highly—and as readily discharged a servant who lied as one who stole. Parents were shocked when they found a child given to lying and made such child the subject of earnest prayer as well as of faithful instruction. The man whose word was as good as his bond was ever honored.

The present descendants of pioneers can best honor the memory of their ancestors by striving to make their homes the abodes of parents and children, who are characterized by the fear and love of God, by the right use of His name, by love for His house and His word, by mutual love of parents and children, by love for the well-being of all others, by purity of life, by honesty, industry, economy and charity, and by truthfulness in all their relations with men.

The glory of our Commonwealth has not been attained alone by the services of men in schools, in churches, in the many departments of industry and in the various branches of civil government. None has rendered more important services than the homes of godly pioneers and their descendants. Good homes make good citizens and these are the strength of the Commonwealth. Men who seek homes for themselves, and men who have secured homes for themselves and their families, are the strongest supporters of good government; law-abiding citizens not through fear, but in view of their respect for constituted authority. With such is not found the initiative step that leads to strikes and the disturbance of social relations in the State. When men pray for the prosperity of the State they should ever pray "God bless our homes," for if these are made by God's favor what they ought to be, then may we hold as true that such is one of God's ways to save the Commonwealth and also the Republic.

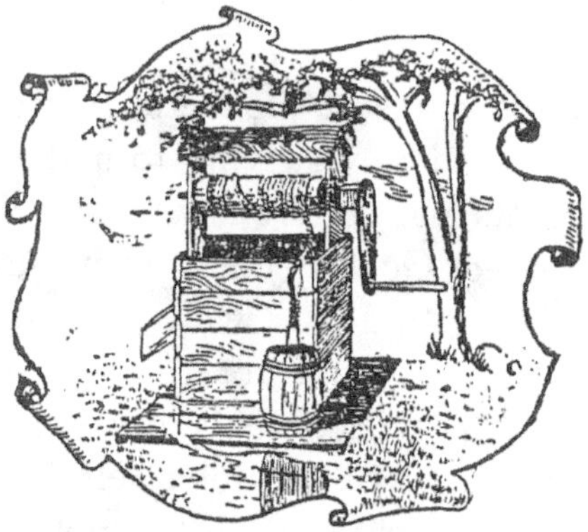

"ALL'S WELL THAT ENDS WELL.

APPENDIX.

CHRISTOPHER DOCK'S ONE HUNDRED NECESSARY RULES OF CONDUCT FOR CHILDREN.[1]

(Translation by Hon. Samuel W. Pennypacker.)

I. Rules for the Behavior of a Child in the House of its Parents.

A. At and after getting up in the mornings.

1. Dear child, accustom yourself to awaken at the right time in the morning without being called, and as soon as you are awake get out of bed without delay.

2. On leaving the bed fix the cover in a nice, orderly way.

3. Let your first thoughts be directed to God, according to the example of David, who says, Psalms cxxxix, 18, "When I am awake I am still with Thee," and Psalms lxiii, 7, "When I am awake I speak of Thee."

4. Offer to those who first meet you, and your parents, brothers and sisters, a good-morning, not from habit simply, but from true love.

5. Learn to dress yourself quickly but neatly.

6. Instead of idle talk with your brothers and sisters or others, seek also, while dressing, to have good thoughts. Remember the clothing of righteousness which was earned

[1] These Rules of Conduct were published about 1764, in Saur's *Geistliches Magazien.* For a full account of Christopher Dock, see Pennypacker's Historical and Biographical Sketches. Philadelphia, 1883.

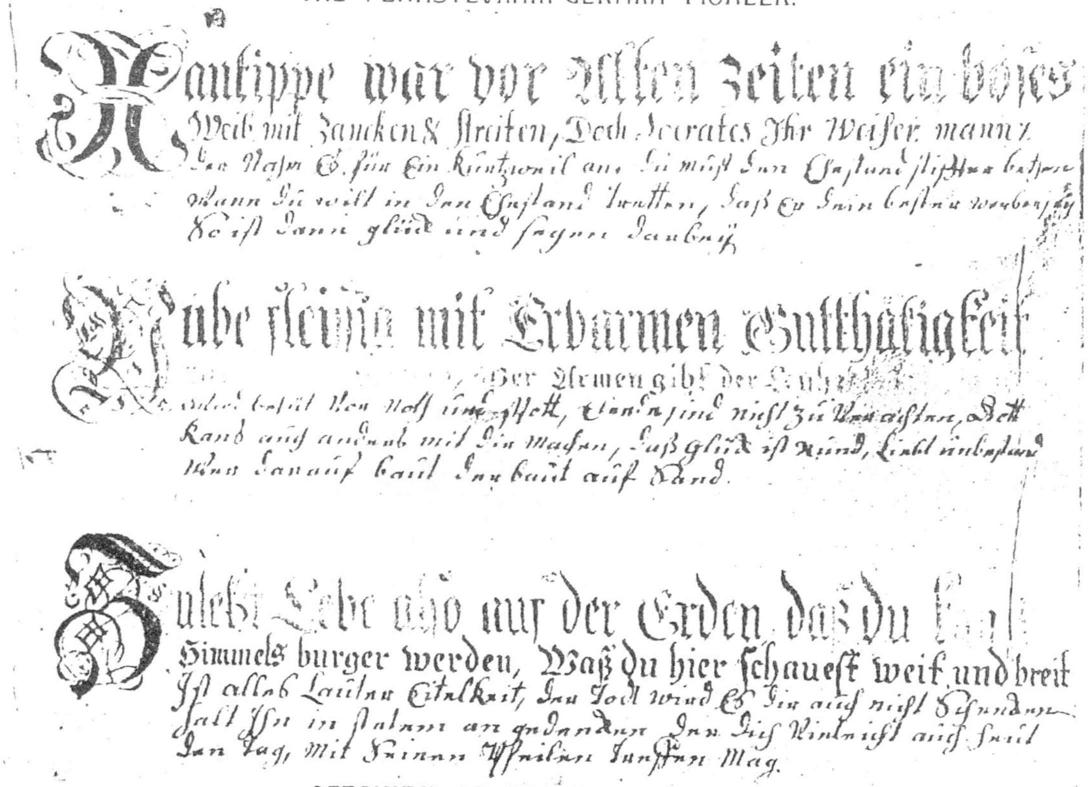

SPECIMEN OF EARLY PENMANSHIP.

ORIGINAL BY CHRISTOPHER DOCK IN HISTORICAL SOCIETY OF PENNSYLVANIA.

for you through Jesus, and form the resolution not to soil it on this day by intentional sin.

7. When you wash your face and hands do not scatter the water about in the room.

8. To wash out the mouth every morning with water, and to rub off the teeth with the finger, tends to preserve the teeth.

9. When you comb your hair do not go out into the middle of the room, but to one side in a corner.

10. Offer up the morning prayer, not coldly from custom, but from a heart-felt thankfulness to God, Who has protected you during the night, and call upon Him feelingly to bless your doings through the day. Forget not the singing and the reading in the Bible.

11. Do not eat your morning bread upon the road or in school, but ask your parents to give it to you at home.

12. Then get your books together and come to school at the right time.

B. In the evenings at bed-time.

13. After the evening meal do not sit down in a corner to sleep, but perform your evening devotions with singing, prayer and reading, before going to bed.

14. Undress yourself in a private place, or if you must do it in the presence of others, be retiring and modest.

15. Look over your clothes to see whether they are torn, so that they may be mended in time.

16. Do not throw your clothes about in the room, but lay them together in a certain place, so that in the morning early you can easily find them again.

17. Lie down straight in the bed modestly, and cover yourself up well.

18. Before going to sleep consider how you have spent

the day, thank God for His blessings, pray to Him for the forgiveness of your sins, and commend yourself to His merciful protection.

19. Should you wake in the night, think of God and His omnipresence, and entertain no idle thoughts.

C. At meal-time.

20. Before going to the table where there are strangers, comb and wash yourself very carefully.

21. During the grace do not let your hands hang toward the earth, or keep moving them about, but let them, with your eyes, be directed to God.

22. During the prayer do not lean or stare about, but be devout and reverent before the majesty of God.

23. After the prayer, wait until the others who are older have taken their places, and then sit down at the table quietly and modestly.

24. At the table sit very straight and still, do not wabble with your stool, and do not lay your arms on the table. Put your knife and fork upon the right and your bread on the left side.

25. Avoid everything which has the appearance of eager and ravenous hunger, such as to look at the victuals anxiously, to be the first in the dish, to tear off the bread all at once in noisy bites, to eat quickly and eagerly, to take another piece of bread before the last is swallowed down, to take too large bites, to take the spoon too full, to stuff the mouth too full, etc.

26. Stay at your place in the dish, be satisfied with what is given to you, and do not seek to have of everything.

27. Do not look upon another's plate to see whether he

has received something more than you, but eat what you have with thankfulness.

28. Do not eat more meat and butter than bread; do not bite the bread off with the teeth; cut regular pieces with the knife, but do not cut them off before the mouth.

29. Take hold of your knife and spoon in an orderly way and be careful that you do not soil your clothes or the table cloth.

30. Do not lick off your greasy fingers, wipe them on a cloth, but as much as possible use a fork instead of your fingers.

31. Chew your food with closed lips and make no noise by scraping on the plate.

32. Do not wipe the plate off either with the finger or the tongue, and do not thrust your tongue about out of your mouth. Do not lean your elbows on the table when you carry the spoon to the mouth.

33. Do not take salt out of the salt-box with your fingers, but with the point of your knife.

34. The bones, or what remains over, do not throw under the table, do not put them on the table cloth, but let them lie on the edge of the plate.

35. Picking the teeth with the knife or fork does not look well and is injurious to the gums.

36. As much as possible abstain from blowing your nose at the table, but if necessity compels, turn your face away or hold your hand or napkin before it; also when you sneeze or cough.

37. Learn not to be delicate and over-nice or to imagine that you cannot eat this or that thing. Many must learn to eat among strangers what they could not at home.

38. To look or smell at the dish holding the provisions too closely is not well. Should you find a hair or some-

thing of the kind in the food, put it quietly and unnoticed to one side so that others be not moved to disgust.

39. As often as you receive anything on your plate, give thanks with an inclination of the head.

40. Do not gnaw the bones off with your teeth or make a noise in breaking out the marrow.

41. It is not well to put back on the dish what you have once had on your plate.

42. If you want something across the table be careful not to let your sleeve hang in the dish or to throw a glass over.

43. At table do not speak before you are asked, but if you have noticed anything good at church or school, or a suitable thought occurs to you relating to the subject of discourse, you may properly bring it forward, but listen attentively to the good things said by others.

44. When you drink you must have no food in your mouth, and must incline forward courteously.

45. It has a very bad look to take such strong draughts while drinking that one has to blow or breathe heavily; while drinking to let the eyes wander around upon others; to commence drinking at table before parents or more important persons have drunk; to raise the glass to the mouth at the same time of one of more importance; to drink while others are speaking to us; and to raise the glass many times after one another.

46. Before and after drinking, the mouth ought to be wiped off, not with the hand but with a handkerchief or napkin.

47. At the table be ready to help others if there is something to be brought into the room or other things to be done that you can do.

48. When you have had enough, get up quietly, take

your stool with you, wish a pleasant meal-time, and go to one side and wait what will be commanded you. Still should one in this respect follow what is customary.

49. Do not stick the remaining bread in your pocket, but let it lie on the table.

50. After leaving the table, before you do anything else, give thanks to your Creator who has fed and satisfied you.

II. Rules for the Behavior of a Child in School.

51. Dear child, when you come into school, incline reverently, sit down quietly in your place, and think of the presence of God.

52. During prayers think that you are speaking with God, and when the word of God is being read, think that God is speaking with you. Be also devout and reverential.

53. When you pray aloud, speak slowly and deliberately; and when you sing, do not try to drown the voices of others, or to have the first word.

54. Be at all times obedient to your teacher, and do not let him remind you many times of the same thing.

55. Should you be punished for bad behavior, do not, either by words or gestures, show yourself impatient or obstinate, but receive it for your improvement.

56. Abstain in school from useless talking, by which you make the work of the schoolmaster harder, vex your fellow pupils, and prevent yourself and others from paying attention.

57. Listen to all that is said to you, sit very straight and look at your teacher.

58. When you recite your lesson, turn up your book

without noise, read loudly, carefully and slowly, so that every word and syllable may be understood.

59. Give more attention to yourself than to others, unless you are placed as a monitor over them.

60. If you are not questioned, be still; and do not help others when they say their lessons, but let them speak and answer for themselves.

61. To your fellow-scholars show yourself kind and peaceable, do not quarrel with them, do not kick them, do not soil their clothes with your shoes or with ink, give them no nick-names, and behave yourself in every respect toward them as you would that they should behave toward you.

62. Abstain from all coarse, indecent habits or gestures in school, such as to stretch with the hands or the whole body from laziness; to eat fruit or other things in school; to lay your hand or arm upon your neighbor's shoulder, or under your head, or to lean your head forwards upon the table; to put your feet on the bench, or let them dangle or scrape; or to cross your legs over one another, or stretch them apart, or to spread them too wide in sitting or standing; to scratch your head; to play or pick with the fingers; to twist and turn the head forwards, backwards and sideways; to sit and sleep; to creep under the table or bench; to turn your back to your teacher; to change your clothes in school, and to show yourself restless in school.

63. Keep you books, inside and outside, very clean and neat, do not write or paint in them, do not tear them, and lose none of them.

64. When you write, do not soil your hands and face with ink, do not scatter it over the table or bench, or over your clothes or those of others.

65. When school is out, make no great noise; in going downstairs, do not jump over two or three steps at a time, by which you may be hurt, and go quietly home.

III. How a Child Should Behave on the Street.

66. Dear child, although, after school, you are out of sight of your teacher, God is present in all places and you therefore have cause upon the street to be circumspect before Him and His Holy Angels.

67. Do not run wildly upon the street, do not shout, but go quietly and decently.

68. Show yourself modest, and do not openly, before other people, what ought to be done in a private place.

69. To eat upon the street is unbecoming.

70. Do not stare aloft with your eyes, do not run against people, do not tread purposely where the mud is the thickest, or in the puddles.

71. When you see a horse or wagon coming, step to one side, and take care that you do not get hurt, and never hang behind upon a wagon.

72. In winter do not go upon the ice or throw snowballs at others, or ride upon sleds with disorderly boys.

73. In summer do not bathe in the water or go too near it. Take no pleasure in mischievous or indecent games.

74. Do not stand in the way where people quarrel or fight, or do other evil things; associate not with evil companions who lead you astray; do not run about at the annual fair; do not stand before mountebanks or look upon the wanton dance, since there you learn nothing but evil.

75. Do not take hold of other children so as to occupy the street, or lay your arm upon the shoulders of others.

76. If any known or respectable person meets you, make way for him, bow courteously, do not wait until he is already near or opposite to you, but show to him this respect while you are still some steps from him.

IV. Rules for the Behavior of a Child in Meeting or Church.

77. Dear child, in meeting or church think upon the holy presence of God, and that you will be judged according to the word you hear upon this day.

78. Bring your Bible and hymn-book with you, and sing and pray very devoutly, since out of the mouths of young children will God be praised.

79. During the sermon be attentive to all that is said, mark what is represented by the text, and how the discourse is divided; which also you can write on your slate. Refer to other beautiful passages in your Bible, but without noise or much turning of the leaves, and mark them by laying in long narrow bits of paper, of which you must always have some lying in your Bible.

80. Do not talk in church, and if others want to talk with you do not answer. During the sermon, if you are overcome with sleep, stand up a little while and try to keep it off.

81. When the name of Jesus is mentioned or used in prayer uncover or incline your head, and show yourself devout.

82. Do not stare about the church at other people, and keep your eyes under good discipline and control.

83. All indecent habits which, under Rule No. 62, you ought to avoid in school, much more ought you to avoid in church.

84. If you, with others should go in couples into, or out of the church you should never, from mischief, shove, tease or bespatter, but go forth decently and quietly.

V. Rules for the Behavior of a Child under various Circumstances.

85. Dear child, live in peace and unity with every one, and be entirely courteous from humility and true love of your neighbor.

86. Accustom yourself to be orderly in everything, lay your books and other things in a certain place and do not let them lie scattered about in a disorderly way.

87. When your parents send you on an errand, mark well the purpose for which you are sent, so that you make no mistake. When you have performed your task come quickly home again and give an answer.

88. Be never idle, but either go to assist your parents, or repeat your lessons, and learn by heart what was given you. But take care that you do not read in indecent or trifling books, or pervert the time, for which you must give an account to God, with cards or dice.

89. If you get any money, give it to some one to keep for you, so that you do not lose it, or spend it for dainties. From what you have willingly give alms.

90. If anything is presented to you, take it with the right hand and give thanks courteously.

91. Should you happen to be where some one has left money or other things lying on the table, do not go too near or remain alone in the room.

92. Never listen at the door, Sirach 21, 24. Do not run in quickly, but knock modestly, wait until you are

called, incline as you walk in, and do not slam the door.

93. Do not distort your face, in the presence of people, with frowns or sour looks; be not sulky if you are asked anything, let the question be finished without your interrupting, and do not answer with nodding or shaking the head, but with distinct and modest words.

94. Make your reverence at all times deeply and lowly with raised face. Do not thrust your feet too far out behind. Do not turn your back to people, but your face.

95. Whether a stranger or good friend comes to the house, be courteous to him, bid him welcome, offer him a chair and wait upon him.

96. In sneezing, blowing the nose, spitting, and yawning be careful to use all possible decency. Turn your face to one side, hold the hand before it, put the uncleanliness of the nose in a handkerchief and do not look at it long, let the spittal fall upon the earth and tread upon it with your foot. Do not accustom yourself to continual hawking, grubbing at the nose, violent panting, and other disagreeable and indecent ways.

97. Never go about nasty and dirty. Cut your nails at the right time and keep your clothes, shoes and stockings neat and clean.

98. In laughing, be moderate and modest. Do not laugh at everything, and especially at the evil or misfortune of other people.

99. If you have promised anything try to hold to it, and keep yourself from all lies and untruths.

100. Let what you see of good and decent in other Christian people serve as an example for yourself. "If there be any virtue, and if there be any praise, think on these things." Philippians iv, 8.

PRIMITIVE PENNSYLVANIA.

SCENE ON THE LEHIGH.

"DER ALT FEUERHERD."

FIREPLACE IN A PROVINCIAL KITCHEN ON THE TULPEHOCKEN, LEBANON CO., PENNA., STILL IN USE.

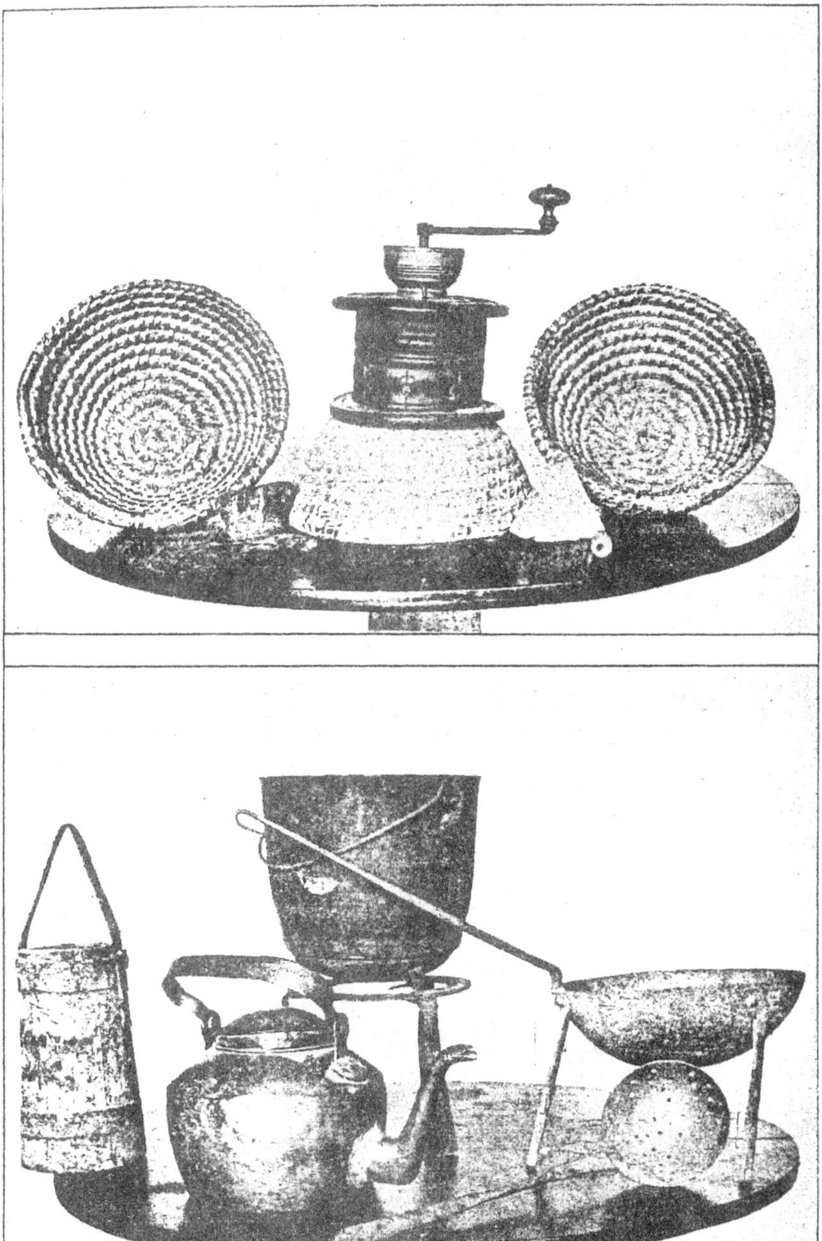

J. F. SACHSE, PHOTO.

DOMESTIC UTENSILS.

(A) BREAD BASKETS, DOUGH-TROUGH SCRAPERS AND COFFEE-MILL.
(B) TAR-BUCKET, TEA-KETTLE, CAULDRON, SKILLET AND SCHAUM-LÖFFELL.

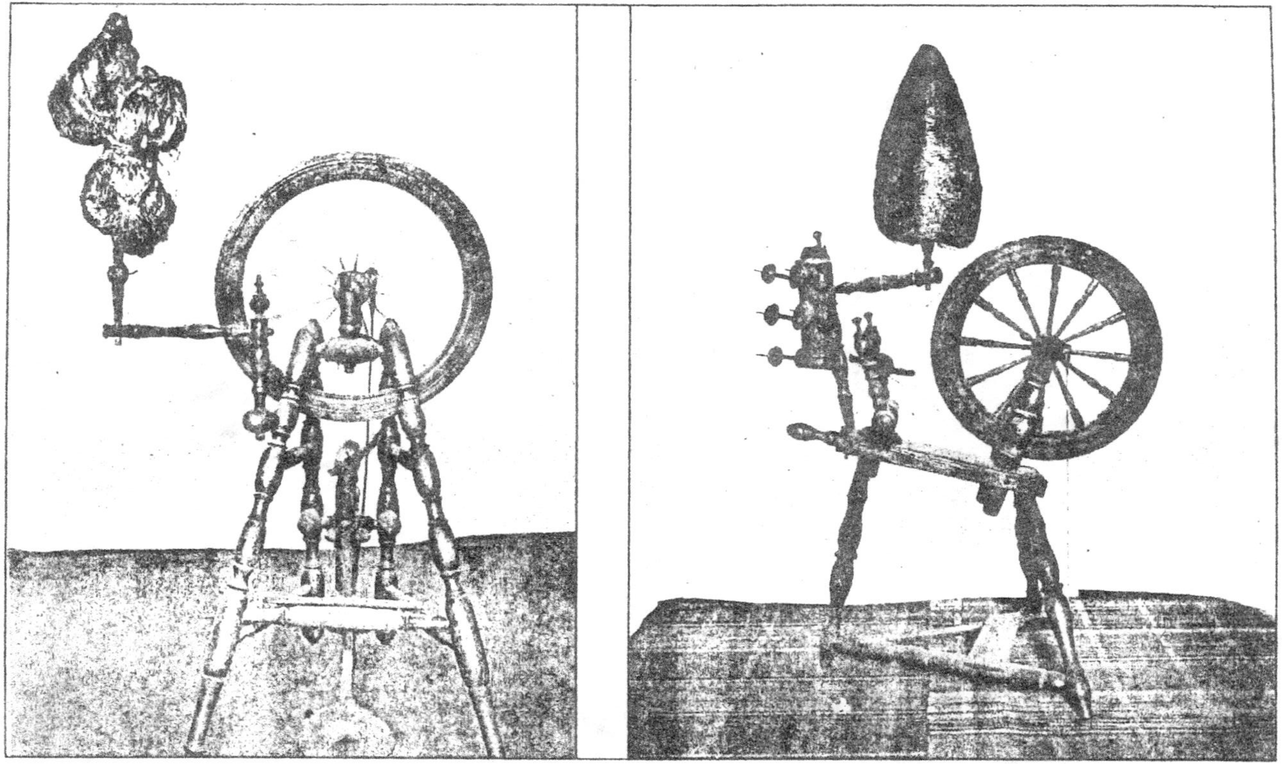

J. F. SACHSE, PHOTO.

DOMESTIC INDUSTRIES.

TYPICAL PENNSYLVANIA-GERMAN SPINNING WHEELS.

ORIGINALS IN DANNER COLLECTION, MANHEIM, PA.

AN OLD PENNSYLVANIA-GERMAN LOOM SHOP.

"DER ALT WEBER-STUHL."

CHARACTERISTICS OF THE PENNSYLVANIA-GERMAN.

PIETY AND INDUSTRY.

BIBLIA,

Das ist:

Die

Heilige Schrifft

Altes und Neues

Testaments,

Nach der Deutschen Uebersetzung

D. Martin Luthers,

Mit jedes Capitels kurtzen Summarien, auch beygefügten vielen und richtigen Parllelen;

Nebst einem Anhang

Des dritten und vierten Buchs Esra und des dritten Buchs der Maccabäer.

Germantown:

Gedruckt bey Christoph Saur, 1743.

TITLE-PAGE OF SAUER BIBLE OF 1743.

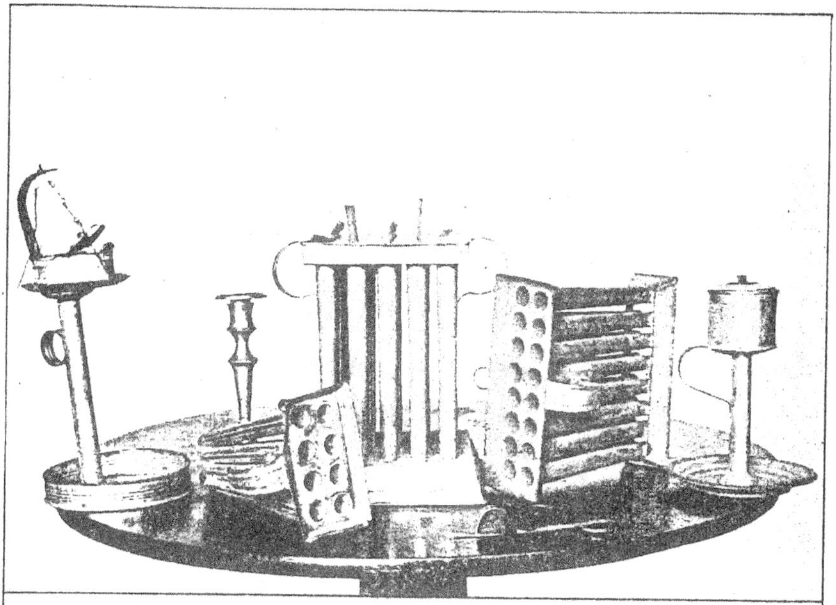

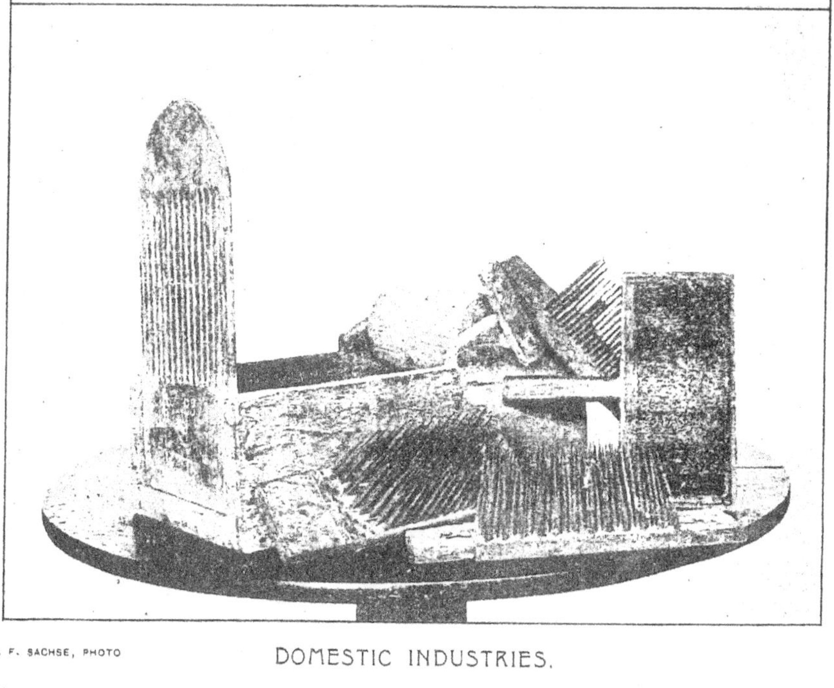

J. F. SACHSE, PHOTO

DOMESTIC INDUSTRIES.

(A) TALLOW CANDLE MOULDS. (B) FLAX HACKLES AND OTHER IMPLEMENTS.

ARRANGED AND PHOTO. BY J. F. SACHSE.

ZINNGESCHIRR (PEWTER TABLE WARE).

USED BY THE GERMANS IN PENNSYLVANIA DURING THE COLONIAL PERIOD.

J. F. SACHSE, PHOTO.

AN OLD COLONIAL HOUSE.

AT THE HEAD OF THE TULPEHOCKEN,—ON THE LEY (URICH) FARM.

Other Heritage Books by Don Heinrich Tolzmann:

Amana: William Rufus Perkins' and Barthinius L. Wick's History of the Amana Society, or Community of True Inspiration

Americana Germanica: Paul Ben Baginsky's Bibliography of German Works Relating to America, 1493–1800

Biography of Baron Von Steuben, the Army of the American Revolution and Its Organizer: Rudolf Cronau's Biography of Baron von Steuben

CD: German-American Biographical Index (Midwest Families)

CD: Germans, Volume 2

CD: The German Colonial Era (four volumes)

Cincinnati's German Heritage

Covington's German Heritage

Custer: Frederick Whittaker's Complete Life of General George A. Custer, Major General of Volunteers, Brevet Major General U.S. Army and Lieutenant-Colonel Seventh U.S. Cavalry

Dayton's German Heritage: Karl Karstaedt's Golden Jubilee History of the German Pioneer Society of Dayton, Ohio

Early German-American Newspapers: Daniel Miller's History

German Americans in the Revolution

German Immigration to America: The First Wave

German Pioneer Life and Domestic Customs

German Pioneer Lifestyle

German Pioneers in Early California: Erwin G. Gudde's History

German-American Achievements: 400 Years of Contributions to America

German-Americana: A Bibliography

Germany and America, 1450–1700

Kentucky's German Pioneers: H. A. Rattermann's History

Lives and Exploits of the Daring Frank and Jesse James: Thaddeus Thorndike's Graphic and Realistic Description of Their Many Deeds of Unparalleled Daring in the Robbing of Banks and Railroad Trains

Louisiana's German Heritage: Louis Voss' Introductory History

Maryland's German Heritage: Daniel Wunderlich Nead's History

Memories of the Battle of New Ulm: Personal Accounts of the Sioux Uprising. L. A. Fritsche's History of Brown County, Minnesota (1916)

Michigan's German Heritage: John Andrew Russell's History of the German Influence in the Making of Michigan

Ohio's German Heritage

Outbreak and Massacre by the Dakota Indians in Minnesota in 1862: Marion P. Satterlee's Minute Account of the Outbreak, with Exact Locations, Names of All Victims, Prisoners at Camp Release, Refugees at Fort Ridgely, etc. Complete List of Indians Killed in Battle and Those Hung, and Those Pardoned at Rock Island, Iowa

The German Element in Virginia: Herrmann Schuricht's History

The German Immigrant in America

The Pennsylvania Germans: James Owen Knauss, Jr.'s Social History

The Pennsylvania Germans: Jesse Leonard Rosenberger's Sketch of Their History and Life